The History Of Rinaldo Rinaldini: Captain Of Banditti, Volume 3

Christian August Vulpius

RINALDO RINALDINI.

Vol. III.

THE
HISTORY

OF

RINALDO RINALDINI,

CAPTAIN OF BANDITTI.

FROM THE GERMAN VULVIUS.

Vulpius, Christian August

IN THREE VOLUMES

VOL. III.

BOSTON:

PRINTED FOR THE BOOKSELLERS.

1832.

FERRANDINO

Loud howled the winds—the waves burst tempestuously upon the shore,—the lightning blazed through the darkness of the clouds; Heaven and earth were in uproar.—Still lay Ferrandino beneath the waving cypresses, and lost in thought, heeded not the raging of the storm.

Not far from Malta stands the little uninhabited island of Lampidosa, gloomy and lonesome, but its secure harbour affords a safe retreat for vessels driven thither by the stress of weather. In the middle of this island is a little chapel, dedicated to the Virgin; none, in quitting the harbour, whether Christian or Mahomedan, omit to leave behind them ammunition or provisions, as a votive offering for the protection they have received. Whosoever needs either, deposits an equivalent in gold; and galleys come from Malta, yearly, to carry the offerings to the chapel of our Lady at Trapani, in Sicily.

Sestoni, the hermit of Lampidosa, was kneeling in prayer before the altar. The rain poured down in torrents; the thunder rolled more heavily, and the earth trembled. Ferrandino sought for shelter and protection in the chapel. Sestoni still knelt in silence before the altar of the Holy One.

A vivid flash of lightning blazed through the chapel, followed by a heavy clap of thunder. The whole building shook—the consecrated lamps clashed together—and the image of the Holy Virgin seemed to totter. Ferrandino started up, and rushed to the door of the chapel. Sestoni followed him.

Sestoni. It is now three years since I fled the society of man, and became a voluntary exile on this desert island; but a storm like this I never witnessed till now

Ferrandino. It is indeed terrible! Wo to those whom it meets upon the sea. It follows all who brave the ocean, however guarded by purity of heart.

Sestoni. But will not injure them.

Ferrandino. Heaven permits the sun to shine upon the just and the unjust, and its lightnings blaze every where.

Sestoni. He who has a pure heart and a clear conscience, may meet the lightning's flash without terror.

Ferrandino sighed heavily.

Sestoni. That sigh, Ferrandino! Does it rise from your fortune or your heart?

Ferrandino. From both!

Sestoni. Strange man! You sailed hither from Malta to give yourself up to religion,—find me, resolve to remain here, renounce the world, and yet seem to cherish a secret desire to mingle with mankind again, which I cannot comprehend. Why. do you not gratify this desire? Why do you not return to the world you have forsaken?

Ferrandino. Who likes to fly towards his pursuers?

Sestoni. If you are indeed pursued, you must either be a man well-known to fame, or a criminal.

Ferrandino. Do you think so?

Sestoni. The celebrated find those who envy them. The criminal find judges.

Ferrandino. And what do you call him who has devoted his heart to love?

Sestoni. A fool, while he does so,—and will be as long as the devotion lasts

Ferrandino. You are no friend to women?

Sestoni. No.

Ferrandino. It is clear then that misanthrophy alone has banished you to this island.

Sestoni And what keeps *you* here?

Ferrandino. The love of solitude.

Sestoni. You are mistaken if you believe that man can any where find a spot, that is real solitude. His heart is with him. If you have left yours with a woman, you may perhaps be solitary, unless any action of your life has roused your conscience to a companion.

Ferrandino. What makes you suppose I have?

Sestoni. I could swear that you have some burthern upon your mind, secret to the world, and therefore the more intolerable to yourself.

Ferrandino. I love my freedom.

Sestoni. And are in love?

Ferrandino. I *was* so!

Sestoni. Who has been? But you *are* so still!

Ferrandino. Do you think so?

Sestoni I will tell you your history in a few words. You are in love with that, which another possesses:—You have murdered—

Ferrandino. Sestoni!

Sestoni. Deny not that which I find legibly written in every feature of your face,— And after all, what is murder?

Ferrandino. Is it the pious, devoted Sestoni, the holy hermit of Lampidosa, that speaks with me!

Sestoni. Who else should it be ? I am not, indeed, speaking of myself.

Ferrandino. Are we not mistaken in each other ?—Sestoni! Sestoni! the thought has already so poisoned my solitude that with the first ship that touches here, I quit the Island.

Sestoni. Whither would you go ?

Ferrandino. To me it is indifferent.

Sestoni. Indeed ! Can you then go *any* where?

Ferrandino. Why not ?

Sestoni. I myself cannot!

Ferrandino. You cannot ?

Sestoni. No! But I can confess it without blushing.

He turned round, and taking up the great altar-lamp, said, quite coolly,

"Heaven rend us fresh oil for this lamp —our stock is almost exhausted."

He returned to the door—and raising his eyes to heaven, sighed loud and deeply. The rage of the tempest began to cease;

the rain did not fall so violently as before, and Ferrandino returned to his dwelling.

About a hundred paces from the chapel where three little hermitages, which, many years before, had been inhabited by three hermits,—a Christian, a Greek, and a Mahomedan, who lived together in perfect concord. The two last died, and were buried near their dwellings. The Christian was the last—a Turkish pirate found him lying dead upon his bed, read his history and that of his companions, which he had left behind; and having burried him, left this account for those that might come after him. These writings. and the simple furniture of a cloister, remained. One of the dwellings Sestoni inhabited; a second Ferrandino: and the third was converted into a store-room.

Ferrandino reached his dwelling, and threw himself thoughtfully on his bed of straw. Here he was still lying, wrapt in meditation, when he was roused from his dream by a gun-shot. He started up, and left his hermitage—Sestoni met him—They looked at each other in silence, and went to the harbour, where all was bustle. A boat put off to the shore. The ship bore French colours, and French-men immediately landed.

Sestoni went to meet them—"Dorval!" exclaimed a Frenchman—and Sestoni sunk into his arms.

Ferrandino drew back, and as nobody seemed to take notice of his presence, retired slowly to his hermitage. Here he waited in vain for Sestoni's return, but the evening came, and he retnrned not—It was night, and still Sestoni did not come—Ferrandino barred the door, and went to rest.

A beautiful morning rose after the storm. Ferrandino awoke and went to Sestoni's dwelling ; He found it empty.

" Propably," thought he, "Sestoni remains on board the ship."

At this instant three signal guns were fired—He hastened to the harbour and saw the ship sailing away. In the chapel he found a letter, in which Sestoni briefly took his leave. Nothing more than this was left behind.

" I have then learnt to know one hypocrite more," said Ferrandino mentally, and returned in a melancholy mood to his cloister.

Four days after, a Sardinian packet, from the Levant, entered the harbour. Ferrandino found the captain a friendly man, and determined to quit the island ; he loft his hermitage, and took his passage with him to Sardinia. Arrived at Cagliari, he took a pleasant lodging in one of the most frequented streets. He visited the church, and the promenades, but found on all sides strange faces, and little entertainment.

He was one day walking round the gardens before the city, according to custom; the evening came on, and he was about to return to his own dwelling, when he chanced to pass by a garden, the door of which stood open ; he stopped, and heard the sound of music, and singing. Curiosity led him to the door—by degrees he went on to the garden. The music and singing now ceased, and soon after a female figure came out of an harbour at the end of the walk and entered the summer-house.

Ferrandino turned round, and was going to leave the garden, when he saw a girl by a flower bed. He spoke to her, and asked her if she would sell the flowers.

"O yes," said the girl, "I am always glad to earn any trifle."

She picked a beautiful nosegay, and Ferrandino paid her well for it. She thanked him, and seeing that he still delayed to go, inquired if he wished for any thing else.

Ferrandino: I should wish to ask you one question.

Girl. Speak then—My father says, he that asks will gain instruction.

Ferrandino. Just now, I saw a lady go out of the arbour into the house. Does this garden belong to her?

Girl. Yes.

Ferrandino. Who is she?

Girl. The lady Fiammetta.

Ferrandino. Is she married?

Girl. No!

Ferrandino. Is she handsome?

Girl. I think so!

Ferrandino. Rich?

Girl. O, yes!

Ferrandino. Independent?

Girl. What do you mean by that?

Ferrandino. Has she parents, sister—?

Girl. That I know not.

Ferrandino. Acquaintances?

Girl. O yes!

Ferrandino. Lovers?

Girl. That question I cannot answer. And if she had, she would not tell me. I am as you know, the daughter of her gardener, but not her confidante. So saying, the girl left him.

Ferrandino was about to go himself, when an old man of dark appearance entered the garden. He received Ferrandino's salutation coldly, and giving him a piercing look, pressed by him towards the summer-house—On a sudden he stopped, and said—

"Are you seeking for any thing here?"

"I have found what I sought," replied Ferrandino, showing him the nosegay.

The old man seemed anxious to inquire farther, but evidently suppressed the half formed question, and went away. Ferrandino walked slowly to the garden door. A sedan chair, borne by two Moors, was set down at the gate; it was opened and a lady came out. Her veil was thrown back, and Ferrandino gazed upon a pair of sparkling eyes, that mocked description. It was as if an electric shock darted through every nerve in his body; he started back a few steps, and taking off his hat, made a low bow, which had evidently no meaning. The lady smiled, returned the compliment, and flew rather than ran down the walk. In her flight, the handkerchief fell from her bosom. Ferrandino picked it up and at first hastened after her, but on the sudden stopped, pressed the handkerchief to his breast, and left the garden.

And now he examined his prize more narrowly. It was a blue silk handkerchief, from which as he examined it, a little written paper, closely rolled up, fell out.

He reflected a moment and delayed to open it.

"What right have I," said he, " to

dive into the secrets of a lady who is un-known to me—But does this letter contain secrets?—How does that concern you—Return her the paper unread; you know her not—Will you be able to find her? And even if you could, will she believe that you have not read that which it was in your power to read? Will she not laugh at you, if she does believe it?"

As he said this, he quickly unfolded the paper, and found a passport, such as Rinaldini, the robber chief, gave to travellers whom he did not wish to be plundered by his people.

He was yet considering the strange passport, when he heard a knocking at the door. He put the letter into his pocket, and the daughter of his landlady entered the room.

"During your absence this letter has been left with us for you," said she, and gave him the paper.

She left the room—He broke open the letter, and read as follows.

"The banker Trivolto informs the Signor Ferrandino, that letters have been left for him at his house.

Ferrandino had scarcely read this, when a Franciscan friar entered his apartment, and announced himself thus:

"God be with you, noble Sir! I am the Father Giovanno, of the order of the holy St. Francis."

Ferrandino. What brings you to me? I am a stranger here——

Giovanno. I know it—What brings me here! My heart, which seeks yours.

Ferrandino. Be more explicit, father.

Giovanno. Permit me then to explain myself. I employ myself with collecting alms from the pious and benevolent—not to enrich myself or my cloister, for our collectors gather the little which is necessary for our support—but to assist the necessitous, who are prevented by sickness or other circumstances, from seeking alms for themselves. Want is ever greatest there, where it presses in silence and in secret. In this pious employment (which by the blessing of God, I have now exercised with singular success for thirteen years) I have by degrees collected a system of remarks, which I intend to leave in writing to whomsoever shall chance to be my successor. Amongst other things, I have observed that strangers are more benevolent than natives; and therefore it is I now apply myself to you—This is what brings me to you; and what I seek from your benevolence. If I do not mistake the character which God has written legibly in your features, my application to you will be successful.

Ferrandino drew a purse of thirty ducats out of his pocket, pressed it into the hand of the humane monk, and said—

"Yes, father, you are right: want, endured in silence and secret, is indeed the greatest. Give this to the poor, whose rank and circumstance will not let them seek for alms themselves, and return if you need my help.

Giovanno. No! I will not abuse your goodness; you have acted so nobly, that this is my first and last application to you— One must not plunder.

Ferrandino. Not so!—You do not plunder me. I therefore again entreat you to return if you need my farther help.

As he said this, he pressed the monk's hand, who said to him in a friendly tone.

"Not so hard! Not so hard! You will break a valuable gift, which I now hold in my hand."

Ferrandino. A valuable gift?
Giovanno. Even so!
Ferrandino. And what is it?
Giovanno. A portrait.
Ferrandino. Of a saint?
Giovanno. (*smiling*) No! It is the portrait of a lady.

Ferrandino.   The portrait of a lady, and in your hands?

Giovanno.   Why not? In my cell I have a collection of pictures, which you may see if you will visit me. Amongst these are many female ones—let me explain this to you—My collection of pictures forms a gallery of almoners. Those who are the most beneficent, I entreat to favour me with their portraits. I hang them in order in my cell, and entertain myself with these, when removed from the society of men. Then I can with certainty say, Now I AM AMONGST MEN. This portrait also shall be added to the gallery. It is the portrait of a noble benefactress.

Saying this, he shewed him the portrait, and Ferrandino recognized in it the likeness of the lady whom he had seen in Fiammetta's garden; the same that had come out of the chair, and in her flight dropped her handkerchief and the robber-passport. Struck by the circumstance, he inquired hastily—" Who is the lady?"

Giovanno.   Does she please you? She has an excellent heart!

Ferrandino,   What is her name?

Giovanno.   She is a stranger, and has been here about six weeks; her name is Fortunata.

Ferrandino. Do you know nothing more of her?

Giovanno. Nothing but what I before said—that she has an excellent heart. But I will not trouble you any longer.

Ferrandino. Not yet!—Let us talk together a while—negotiate—.

Giovanno. Negotiate!—You with me! (*smiling.*) You would not play me any trick, surely?

Ferrandino. Here are thirty ducats more for your indigent, if you will leave me this portrait.

The friar eyed him doubtfully, and said with caution—"I will get the portrait copied for you, if the Signora Fiammetta will give me leave."

"This is to tedious for me," interrupted Ferrandino "I feel interested in the original"

Giovanno. In my gallery you will find many other portraits that will interest you.

Ferrandino, You deprive the poor of thirty ducats—In the future you will receive nothing from me for your alms, unless you leave me this portrait.

Giovanno. You are very resolute—You shall have the portrait,—but under two conditions. You shall let it be copied, and not say that you had it from me.

Ferrandino. I pledge my word for this; and here are the thirty ducats. But now tell me, where does the original of this portrait dwell?

Giovanno. The Signora Fortunata lives in yonder street, at the corner house with the red window-shutters.

Ferrandino now occupied himself with the purchased portrait, and the good hearted father left him.

The following morning Ferrandino fetched his letters from the banking house of Trivolto the banker who proved to be a very unaffected, friendly man. Afterwards he went to the Cathedral, heard a Mass, and then went in search of the corner house, with the red window-shutters. This he found without difficulty, and inquired of a fruit woman "Who dwelt in the house?"

" A foreign lady hired it two months ago, and inhabits it with all her people," was the answer.

In the mean time the two Moors came out of the house with the sedan chair, and Ferrandino followed them at a distance. The chair stopped at a church, was opened, and Fortunata came out.

She went into the church—Ferrandino followed quickly after her—She kelt in prayer—He watched her with a palpitating heart.

When she left the pew, he approached her, and offered her with trembling hand the holy water and stammered—

"I restore to you, Madam, the veil, which you dropped yesterday, when I had the good fortune to meet you in the garden of the Signora Fiammetta."

She smiled, took the veil in silence and thanked him with a courtesy—He led her to the sedan, which she immediately entered and was borne back to her house.

Ferrandino again visited Fiammetta's garden, bought flowers as before, and returned in a melancholy mood to his apartment. At the door he met father Giovanno, who had been waiting for him as he said, and who now followed him to his chamber.

"My son," began the friar; "I come from the lady Fortunata, and have been speaking with her of you. I could not withhold from her the account of your purchasing the portrait, and in the course of our conversation it came out that you had spoken to her this morning, and restored to her a lost veil. All this combined, has made her observe you attentively, and she wishes to see and speak with you this evening.'

Ferrandino embraced the monk in raptures, and enriched his alms-chest with a few ducats. An hour was fixed for the visit, and the father left the delighted Ferrandino.

For a long time the hours had not passed so slowly with him as they did this day. The evening was yet far off and he went to Fiammetta's garden.

He passed through the great walk, entered a by-path, and came at length to a pavilion. The door was half open; he approached it, and saw within an interesting female face. The girl was sitting upon a sofa, and amused herself with weaving a garland of flowers. She saw him, and smiling quite unconcerned, cried out.

"Come in."

Ferrandino in confusion moved the door but yet did not venture to open it entirely, when he was bid a second time in a friendly voice to come in. This gave him courage, and he entered the pavilion.

"I think," said the lady, "I have seen you in my garden twice before."

"Indeed," stammered Ferrandino, "I was here yesterday, and also again this morning; *but I did not indeed expect that I should have the fortune to be observed by such beautiful eyes.*"

The Lady. And why not? As you

have paid a compliment to my beautiful eyes permit me to pay one to your beautiful figure—A man like you, will always be observed. And I would wager, that I am not the first in the world, who has remarked you—Are you a stranger here?

Ferrandino. I am.

Lady. I also am a stranger here—I have lived in this country for these six week, but I hope to become at home, and have therefore purchased this garden

Ferrandino. The garden is beautiful, but the possessor is—

Lady.—Is more beautiful!—That is very natural—May I ask your name?

Ferrandino. Ferrandino.

Lady. Merely Ferrandino? Nothing more? No Count, Marquis, or title of any kind?

Ferrandino. No!—Simply Ferrandino!

Lady. Your pardon! where born?

Ferrandino. I am by birth a——a Maltese.

Lady Indeed! Are you a knight in conito?

Ferrandino. By no means—I am a man who live upon my fortune, and take a delight in living sometimes here and sometimes there.

Lady, That is the case with me

There was now a pause, Ferrandino
gazed earnestly on his fair companion, and
she continued very assiduously at her
work, without once lifting up her eyes.
For a long time he observed her in silence,
and was at last about to speak, when a girl
entered the pavilion and brought Fiammetta a note. She read it and with a smile
wrote a few words on the back, folded it
up again, and returned it to the girl, who
left the pavilion. Fiammetta laid her work,
which was now finished, upon the sofa,
and got up from her seat. As she moved,
a portrait, suspended about her neck by a
green ribbon, slipped out of her bosom, and
hung down. She observed it, and hastily
replaced the minature.

"That was a bad man," said she, "and
his portrait is not for the eyes of every one."

Ferrandino sood before her in speechless
astonishment——Fiammetta turned round
quite unconcerned, as if she had been alone,
walked a few turns about the chamber, sang
and at length took up her guitar.

"She has at length found him out,"
said Fiammetta.

"*We* have found out each other;" exclaimed Ferrandino hastily, and seized her
hand.

"Not exactly so," replied Fiammetta,

laughing, while she gently withdrew her hand. "I am not a gipsey, nor are you a captain of banditti; I cannot tell fortunes, and you will hardly plunder me—"

She seemed as if she would have spoken farther, when an officer entered the pavilion. He saluted Ferrandino coldly, placed his hat and sword upon the table, and sat himself down on the sofa, by the side of Fiammetta with as much ease and coolness as if he had been alone in the chamber. He asked—"Has any thing happened?"

"Nothing of consequence," was the answer, and delivered in the same familiar manner.

The officer now said in an under tone "Who is this gentleman?"

"A stranger," replied Fiammetta.

"Will you not take a seat?" said the officer; but in a tone more suited to the question—"will you go now?"—and that really Ferrandino's intention, when the man with the dark features, whom he had met in the gardens the day before, on a sudden entered the pavilion. He did not salute Ferrandino, but kept on his hat and sat down in a chair opposite to him. staring at him full in the face, he said—

"I observed you yesterday with grief

and wonder—You have an unlucky face."

Ferrandino drew back in terror—Fiammetta and the officer laughed—The physiognomist very deliberately took snuff.

" What has my face done to you ?" said Ferrandino, confused.

" Not that, which it has done to you," replied the old man.

" It is the custom of this gentleman," said Fiammetta, "to say unpleasant things to every body. He is not indeed an Englishman, but yet he has the spleen. The English have inoculated the Corsicans with this disease."

" Are you a Corsican then ?" said Ferrandino, hastily.

" I am," replied the rough old man— "but that cannot concern you at all."

Fiammetta rose up hastily, and taking Ferrandino by the hand, said—

" Take your leave of these gentlemen. We must speak together upon other subjects than Corsica."

Upon this she took him out of the pavilion, and led him round the parterre' to a neighbouring arbour, and in this sat Fortunata.

Ferrandino had left an unentertaining conversation, and now stood before a beautiful woman, whose portrait he so dearly purchased; the very woman, whom he had expected to speak with a few hours after in her own house; and whom he now unexpectedly met with in a place which might have been the point of explanation between him and a lovely female, had not another intervened. All this, to him at least, was so strange and so unexpected, that he could not but feel confused.

Fiammetta flew to the beautiful Fortunata, embraced and kissed her, and Ferrandino thus received time to collect himself.

But he was not long suffered to remain so; Fiammetta turned quickly round, and taking him by the hand, thrust him towards her friend. Ferrandino was confused—Fiammetta laughed aloud, and said;

"There—You have him."

Thus saying, she ran out of the arbour.

Ferrandino stepped back a few paces, and would have spoken but could not. Fortunata looked down upon the ground and played with her handkerchief. Ferrandino thought it was the same, that he had found and restored to her in the morning.

After a long pause he ventured to address her.

Ferrandino. In reality—this scene—

Fortunata. It is strange enough!

Ferrandino. My confusion—

Fortunata. And mine too!—Fiammetta's so wild a creature!—

Ferrandino. I should have had the pleasure of seeing you this evening in your own house, and now fortune comes before the time.

Fortunata. Strange that it should have happened so!

He was about to answer, when Fiammetta entered the arbour.

"I wished," said she, " to entertain you, dear friend, and this gentleman at my house this evening, but it cannot be done. The surly Corsican has invited a party thither to-night."

"Hither," cried Fortunata, hastily.

"Even so," continued Fiammetta; "and I must, whether I will or no, play the hostess this evening—You know how that is. Some guests are already come."

Fortunata rose up quickly and whispered something in Fiammetta's ear; she then turned towards Ferrandino, entreated him to lend his arm, and lead her to her chair. Fiammetta accompanied both to the garden-door, and when Fortunata was gone, seized him by the hand, and said, laughing;

"Now we have got rid of her, and you remain here."

"As you expect company—" stammered Ferrandino, I—.

Fiammetta. Not so—The story of the company was but a jest. It now rests with yourself, either to stay here or to follow her chair.

Ferrandino. I do not comprehend you.

Fiammetta. That is strange! But to speak more plainly! This moment decides for me or for my friend—There is no unkindness nor malice in the affair. But as we wish to know whether you really are what we suppose you to be—

Ferrandino. And what do you suppose me to be?

Fiammetta. A gallant adventurer at least if not a——

Ferrandino. What?

Fiammetta.—A man who can love from the very bottom of his heart.

Ferrandino. Beautiful Fiammetta!

Fiammetta. Away! Away! Follow the chair. This serious tone tells me all I wish to know—Go!—carry this kiss to my friend, and say to her—'Fiammetta has resigned'—God be with you!—May you be happy and remember me!

Upon this, she kissed him forced him gently towards the garden door, and without once looking round ran up the walk to the arbour. Ferrandino saw her flight without emotion, and drawing his hat over his eyes, hastened after the chair. In the city he came up with it, and opened the door to Fortunata, who met him with a smile, and led him to her chamber.

And now they entered into conversation about Fiammetta and her disposition ; and from this he began to speak of her commission,

"She is very good," said Fortunata, "and I shall do all, that she has assigned me."

Ferrandino received a kiss, and Fortunata left the chamber, to dress herself, as she said.

In the mean time Ferrandino began to consider where he was. He now saw what he had not before observed, that he was in a chamber very splendidly furnished. All that he saw evinced taste and fortune, united with more than common splendour

He was looking at an historic picture, when Fortunata entered the room. She had on a beautiful dress thrown—over her shoulders. Ferrandino looked astonished —She took him by the hand, and led him into another chamber much superior to the first.

In this room they entered into a very interesting conversation, which was soon interrupted, by the information, that supper was ready. Ferrandino was now led into a very splendid eating-room, and sat down with his beautiful hostess to a rich repast; two lovely girls waited upon them. The conversation was sprightly, the glasses were quickly emptied, and when the desert was brought in, the waiting women retired.

"I love," said Fortunata, "The pleasures of conversation at a good repast, yet only when I share them with a friend. Since I have lived here, in Cagliari, I have for the most part taken my meals alone, if Fiammetta's society be excepted. To-day I have relished every thing more than usual, and if you intend to stay long in Cagliari, I shall hope to have often the pleasure of your company."

As she said this, she filled a glass and offered it to Ferrandino, with the toast— "To our friendship."

"A pleasant union," she continued, "has been formed by it to-day, and I trust it will subsist for ever."

Ferrandino kissed her hand in silence, and placed it on his beating heart. Their eyes darted looks of eloquence at each other, and their lips met. They were overpowered by their feelings—no sound escaped their lips. On a sudden the cork flew out of a bottle of Champaigne, with a loud noise upon the table—Both laughed at their transient terror, and they lay folded in each others arms.

Fortunata. Man! to whom I have so quickly yielded in the first moments of our acquaintance—I know not what it is that leads me to you so irresistibly.

"O, misuse not the power, which something to me inexplicable, gives you over me! You may make me unhappy, but cannot by that cause happiness to yourself—I know, I feel, what you now perhaps think of me, what you *must* think of me—but I swear to you, you are mistaken—You know not what—

Ferrandino. Fortunata! Let me say that to you, which you have said to me. I shall not let suspicion make me unhappy: only do not you let reality sport at my expense.

Fortunata. You believe then—

Ferrandino. I am always most ready to believe that, which I wish to believe.

Fortunata. What do you now believe?

Ferrandino That you will love me!

Fortunata. I loved you the moment that

I saw you. Love such as mine both gives and takes in a moment. The moment for my love is come, is fixed, and will be so to eternity. By all that is holy in heaven and earth! I have found you, and will never leave you—I must be *forced* from you Never will I willingly relinquish what I now embrace with so much fire in my arms!—My form has delighted you,—I love you *altogether*. Give yourself entirely to me, and in return take all that is mine, except yourself. I yield you my *soul* in my kisses—give me *your heart*.

A noise in the antichamber parted them. The table was now taken away and they went into the next chamber.

Ferrandino threw himself thoughtfully upon a sofa. He was so near the desired fortune and thought upon the possibility of the truth, which he desired. Every other thought was swallowed up in Fortunata. She was born for love.

Love is a glass filled with sparkling wine; it must be enjoyed on the moment. He who drinks deliberately may perhaps enjoy it, but will never know its transports.

It was midnight, and the lovers lay locked in each other's arms, when they were awakened by the dazzling of a light, and a loud shriek. The two maids who h

waited at table stood trembling before the
bed with candles in their hands and cried—

"Ah! What can be the meaning of
this? The house is beset with soldiers."

Fortunata started from the bed, exclaim-
ing—

"The barbarians! Do they follow me every where? Why have they not murdered
me too?"

"Be at ease, Fortunata," said Ferrandino; "That which you imagine concerns
yourself is meant for me."

Fortunata. You? No! No! Nobody is
in pursuit of you!—

Ferrandino. Who then persues you?
You have no enemy that equal mine!—oh!
why did I not remain in the island of Lampidosa.

Fortunata. No, Ferrandino! I know
but too well that it concerns me. You
know not who I am, nor what I was.

Ferrandino. You say precisely that
which I would say.

Fortunata. Does a *king* pursue you?

In the mean time there was a violent
knocking at the street door. Fortunata,
almost beside herself, opened the window,
and cried—

"Who's there?"

"The Viceroy's watch," was the answer

"You are commanded to open the door in the king's name."

"It shall be done immediately," said Fortunata, recovering herself, and closed the window again. She sent the maids down, and ordered them to open the door.

When they had left the chamber, she took up a little casket and gave it to Ferrandino. She then led him up a gallery, opened a window-shutter, and bade him get out upon the balcony; from thence he might leap down into the court and then steal out of the house through a little back gate, the key of which she gave him.

"Farewell! and think of me," she said, kissed him, weeping, and hurried back to her bed-chamber.

Ferrandino did not hesitate long. He ventured the leap, and came safely down into the court. With little difficulty he opened the door, found the street, and got back without being once stopped, to his own dwelling.

The day began to break, and still he had not slept. Towards the morning he had at length fell into a profound slumber, from which, a short time after, he was awakened by a loud knocking at the door. With a trembling voice he inquired who was there, and received for answer, the father

Giovanno. He opened the door, and the friar entered the apartment. He trembled violently, and seating himself, gazed a while at Ferrandino, unable to speak.

Ferrandino. Father! What is the matter with you?

Giovanno. Do you ask? Fortunata bids me greet you.

Ferrandino. Where is she?

Giovanno. I know not where she now is. Two hours ago she was brought into the harbour, and has probably been shipped off with her companions.

Ferrandino. With her companions!

Giovanno. With Fiammetta, and some other Corsicans who have been arrested on our island. It has been done at the desire of the king of France—I know not to what place they will lead them now; probably to France.—Since you have this time escaped the vigilance of the police——

Ferrandino. I am not a Corsican.

Giovanno. No! So much the better then for you. And yet I suspected that you were—for Fortunata said to me—'Tell Ferrandino to be careful of his safety.'— Probably her friendship for you has made her say so from excess of caution.

Ferrandino. But what evil have the Corsicans to Fortunata done?

Giovanno. These are political affairs, about which I do not trouble myself.

Ferrandino. Although I am not a Corsican, and in this respect have nothing to fear for my safety, yet this event has made my abode at Cagliari disagreeable to me. I am therefore resolved to leave the city, and go to some other country. Have you not friends in any country to whom you can give me letters of recommendation?

Giovanno. My elder brother lives here in the king's service. My second brother is a sea-captain, and has his fixed dwelling at Oristagni, but is commonly at sea.— His wife and children, however, live at Oristagni. I have also a sister there, who is the abbess of St. Clara's convent, but her society will not be much satisfaction to you, for she is always ill. If you wish however, to have letters to my sister and and my sister-in-law, you may have them. Oristagni is an agreeable, friendly place, and you will be well pleased there, I have no doubt.

Ferrandino. Give me the letters; I will go to Oristagni.

Giovanno. Am I to call you in my letters, simply Ferrandino?

Ferrandino. Simply Ferrandino. I am a traveller, live upon my fortune, and am by birth a Sicilian.

Giovanno A Sicilian !—Is it long since you left Sicily ?

Ferrandino. Half a year.

Giovanno. Can you tell me the end of the robber-chief, Rinaldini ?

Ferrandino. Only that which all Sicily tells. He fell on the island of Pantalaria by the dagger of one of his friends.

Giovanno. His death is so reported here—You do not, perhaps, know that this man interests me particularly.

Ferrandino. You interested in the fate of Rinaldini ?—Indeed !—Why so ?

Giovanno. For the sake of a friend, who knew him intimately.

Ferrandino. Knew him intimately !—And he lives here ?

Giovanno. He lives as a hermit in a little forest on a small estate, an hour's walk from the city, which some years ago a pious countess presented to our monastery. He often visits me, and we have talked together for hours merely about Rinaldini.

Ferrandino. And this hermit knew him intimately ?

Giovanno. Yes ! Donato knew him intimately.

Ferrandino. Is the hermit's name Donato ?—I must, I will visit him. I also like to hear speak of Rinaldini.—The letters, then, to Oristagni—

Giovanno. I will write them now, in your apartment.

The friar sat down and wrote—Ferrandino walked up and down the chamber thoughtfully.

A knocking was heard at the door—Ferrandino exclaimed, and with beating heart—" Come in—"

One of the two Moors in Fortunata's service entered the room. He looked significantly at Ferrandino, who led him into the next apartment. The monk continued writing, and seemed to take no notice of any thing about him.

The Moor, in the mean time, gave Ferrandino a letter. He opened, and read—

" I have found means to free myself from the intended journey to France. While my companions are carried thither, a passage-boat conveys me in safety to the island of Rossa. I shall find means of going from thence to the island Elba. If you will follow me, you must wait for me six weeks on that island. I am then resolved to go to Minorca. You will at all events retain in your service the bearer of this letter, *Berisso*, a faithful servant. If you really love me, I shall not need to entreat you a second time to follow me. You know how entirely I am yours,

Fortunata.'

Ferrandino now returned to the monk
He had written the letters; and was forced
to leave him hastily, on business respecting his monastery, as he said. They
promised to speak with each other again
before Ferrandino left the country, and the
friar went away.

When he was gone, Ferrandino told the
Moor that he should retain him in his service.

Berisso. But we are going to follow my
noble lady?

Ferrandino. Certainly!—Tell me how
she escaped.

Berisso That I know not—But this I
know—She and Fiammetta spoke for a
long time together with an officer, and
they appeared to know each other. She
gave me a sign privately, and this letter,
with which I flew to you.

Ferrandino. You must hire a calash—
To-morrow we shall travel after her.

It was done—and the following day,
they came to Oristagni.

Scarcely had the day broken, than Ferrandino hurried to the harbour to seek for
a vessel that might take him in pursuit of
Fortunata. He was standing near one of
the watch-towers, and had just given something to a beggar who clamoured loudly

for alms, when a man of large stature, and clothed in a red mantle, placed himself in his way. Ferrandino sought to avoid him, but the man still flung himself in his path.

"What is the meaning of this?" asked Ferrandino.

"You shall not go to the harbour!" was the answer.

"Who are you?"

"A Man!"

"Who gives you right and power to stop me?"

"I give it myself,—for your advantage."

"For my advantage?"

"You would look about in the harbour for a passage boat to carry you to Elba, where an alluring Syren waits for you. It is not well for you to follow her enticing tones.—You must remain in Oristagni— Others know better how to take care of you, than you would of yourself."

"You wrong the lady, of whom you speak."

"I cannot enter into explanations, nor is this the place for them—I will speak to you in your own chamber."

The man in the red mantle went, and Ferrandino took his way to the harbour— The other turned round, called after him, and threatened him with his finger. Ferrandino bethought himself a while. At last he turned round, and went back to his own apartment.

Upon his entrance, Berisso gave him a letter, which, he said, had been given him, by an unknown person.

He broke open the letter, and read as follows:

"It will be much better for you to go over Algeri to Sassari, than to stay here—You will, no doubt, follow the advice of a friend, and not obstinately plunge yourself into danger."

Ferrandino appeared to be brought a little to himself by this letter; he went out and bought a couple of horses—The following morning he set out with Berisso upon his journey.

Towards the mid-day, the air was sultry and oppressive. The sky was overcast; lightnings pierced through the darkness of the heavens; the thunder rolled heavily at a distance—A death-like silence reigned around.

The travellers galloped quickly forwards, and just as a violent shower of rain began to fall, they reached a castle which was situated upon a height They were admitted—Their horses were led into a stall, and they were told that they were in the castle of the Countess Orana, who was then living there. Ferrandino's arrival was announced to her, and she requested the presence of her guest.

She was a woman of understanding, and her conversation with Ferrandino was lively and interesting. She had been, as she said, a widow for two years.—She was still in her prime, and was firmly resolved to retain her freedom and never marry again; —She must, as she expressed it, be conquered by something far more interesting than men usually were. To her other qualifications, that of a poetess was added, and she had composed a satire upon men; but when her guest politely requested to see it, he was refused: at the same time she declared that she received much pleasure from his company, and requested him to stay with her a few days. This, Ferrandino could not refuse.

A female cousin was living with her, whose vivacity added fresh entertainment to the evening meal; Ferrandino had to contend with two ladies, who appeared to be very systematic man-haters—He had never before met with such women.

To turn the scales a little against the ladies, he told them that he was resolved to take the Maltese Cross, because he could not convince himself that any tender union, with a woman could be happy—The scene was now changed; they endeavoured to convince him to the contrary, and the contest lasted till midnight.

A chambermaid now showed Ferrandino his bed-chamber, fitted up in a style of elegance and splendor.

It was late in the morning when he awoke, and he found, the ladies already at breakfast.

At this moment a band of travelling Spanish dancers arrived. They entered the castle hall; the spectators took their places and the music began to play, when a young man and a beautiful girl came in to dance the Bolero.

Both were clothed in a light, Andaulusian dress, invented purposely for the dance;—they hastened together as if they had sought and found each other—And now the young man attempted to embrace his beloved, she seemed ready to rush into his arms, when she suddenly turned round; he as if half angry, did the same—The music made a pause—Both seemed irresolute, but the music began again, again carried them away with it—The youth sought to express his wishes more warmly, and his beloved seemed to listen more tenderly. Her eyes became more languishing, her bosom heaved more frequently, her arms were stretched out towards his—in vain : she retreated, but the pause gave both fresh strength—again the music sounded, and their steps became quicker. Maddened with desire, the young man hastened again to the maiden and she now met him with equal feelings—Their looks were intermingled, their lips seemed to open, but shame still held them back—The music sounded more loudly, and their emotions increased. A transport of voluptuousness seemed to unite them both ; every muscle seemed to swell, every look to melt into pleasure—On a sudden the music was silent, and the dancers vanished.

The cousin cast her eyes on the ground, and played with a nosegay in her breast. The countess turned towards Ferrandine with a smile, and said—

" What do you think of the dance."

" I think, that it is a very enchanting dance."

" Do you think so ?"

" Must not a dance, that speaks in so lively a way to a feeling, that lives in all nature, and alone can soften man ; must not such a dance be more fascinating than any other?"

"O you men," said the countess, smiling, and left the hall.

The cousin got up and followed her, but said as she went—

"Should you not like to know the female dancer more intimately?"

Ferrandino laughed, and approached the travellers.

"Sir," said the dancer; "you seem to be a noble minded man; take this woman under your protection. She needs such a protector."

Ferrandino asked him what he meant; the dancer replied;

"These musicians have played to such dances to-day for the last time. They are engaged by the viceroy, and are about to enter his service; I shall go with them as a flute-player. Thus this maiden will be left in want; you see she is pretty,—Take her with you—"

"How can I do that? I am a traveller, a stranger."

"She is accustomed to travelling and will travel with you."

Ferrandino looked at the girl in silence. She smiled and cast her eyes on the ground. At this moment the Countess entered the hall, and inquired;

"What is the matter here?"

Ferrandino answered earnestly ;

"I have engaged this maiden."

The Countess laughed aloud, and said in an under tone ;

"Whither ?"

Ferrandino without confusion, and very dryly, replied ;

"To my companions and fellow travellers."

"Indeed! My cousin must know that."

The cousin came, and the Countess told her laughing, Ferrandino's intention—The cousin turned to the dancer, and said,

"You will go with this man ?"

"Why not ?" replied the other, with great naivete.

"You do not know who he is."

"Do you then know ?" asked Ferrandino, quickly.

"O yes!" answered the cousin, in the same tone.

Ferrandino looked round him in astonishment—the women laughed aloud. The musicians and the dancer left the hall.

The cousin took the dancer by the hand, led her to Ferrandino, and said ;

"There is the bride—Take her to your den."

Ferrandino stared at her, and would have asked her meaning, when she held a miniature before his eyes. He cast a look at it, and trembling violently started a few steps back.

"Have you," said the cousin, "read the writing beneath this portrait?—It is the likeness of

RINALDIN the ROBBER CHIEF!"

BOOK II

She still continued with unchanging countenance to hold the miniature before him—Ferrandino at length recovered himself—

"I have seen Rinaldini," he said, "but he looked not thus."

"Who knows how he might have painted and disguised himself, when you saw him?—This is his real likeness."

"No! Rinaldini looked not so!—The features of this portrait resemble me—Who has written the name of the robber-chief under this portrait?"

"A person, who knew him well.—Should you like to speak with him?"

"He has lied! This is *my* likeness, and I am not what you imagine me to be!"

The cousin put the picture in his hand with emotion, and said,

"Do not destroy this picture—It is the general belief here, that it is the likeness of the redoubted Rinaldini, and *you* resemble it *much*."

"Had Rinaldini brothers?" said the Countess, confused.

"Many as it is reported—He, himself was murdered at Pantalaria."

The well known man in the red mantle now entered the room. He bowed to the ladies, and then turning to Ferrandino, said ;

At length, Marquis, I have found you. The Viceroy has sent you this equipage, and expects to see you as soon as possible ; there is his letter to you.

Ferrandino opened the letter and read.

Follow me immediately—You can take the girl with you—As to the Moor, Berrisso, do not trouble yourself about him."

In the castle court, a coach with six horses was waiting for him ; the coachmen and outriders were richly habited.—The Countess and her cousin cast a look at the equipage in the castle court, and then gazed at each other with astonishment.

Ferrandino took his leave—The ladies in confusion wished him a happy journey, but yet the Countess did not forget to ask

"Shall you take the tender Bolero dancer with you to the Viceroy ?"

Ferrandino took the maiden by the hand and said;

"You will follow me, whither I am going ?"

He hastened into the castle-court, where he found every thing ready; aud he took the girl with him into the coach. He gave a passing compliment to the ladies, and the carriage rolled away.

In a little wood, where the road divides, the man in the red mantle came up with him.

"We must now change places," said he. "Here is your horse, and a mule for your companion· I shall travel forward in the Viceroy's equipage, and you must strike into the road over the mountains. In a valley, a short distance from hence you will find a little country house, where you will be hospitably received. You must remain there till you see me again,"

"How am I," said Ferrandino; "to learn your name? If your mission to me is really pure, give me some proofs of it— Who are you ?"

"I am called Sanardo—and will give you the proofs you require."

He drew him aside, and took a dagger from his breast.

When Ferrandino saw the dagger, he pressed his hand, and said;

"I have what I desired."

Sanardo got into the carriage, and went away—Ferrandino mounted his horse, his companion her mule, and they took the appointed way. They soon reached the country house that had been described to them, and dismounted. The possessor of it, a man stricken in years, came out to meet them with his wife, who though old. was still lively and in good health.

The servants took their luggage and led the horse and mule to the stable, while, they were conducted into a small chamber, which opened into a second. Here, they found a few books, a guitar, and materials for writing. Their host and hostess, the old Lorenzo and his wife Madalena received them with much hospitality, and with friendly readiness anticipated all their wishes as well as they were able. Ferrandino found solitude very tolerable, and his companion Ersilia appeared to be very well pleased with her present situation. Her lively disposition ever afforded entertainment, and chased melancholy from the cloudy brow of her companion.

"One must," she said, "in this world, consider every moment as lost, that does not offer some enjoyment; he who gives way to melancholy, actually dedicates himself to a living death—Let us, my friend, live for enjoyment.

Ferrandino. Have you no regard to the future?

Ersilia. Has then the future any for me?—Enough for existence is always to be found—and if we rightly consider, what is there more in this world than mere existence. From youth upwards I have been the sport of chance. I have learnt little; my Bolero-dance has hitherto supported me. A thousand times I seemed to sink into the arms of my partner in the dance, and yet, when it was ended, I no more sunk into his arms than I did then—Ferrandino has never danced with me, and yet his arms so tenderly entwine me.

Ferrandino. And suppose I should cease to do so?

Ersilia. Then another would.

Ferrandino, Ersilia speaks with much lightness?

Ersilia. As naturally as she thinks.

She smiled, and, taking up the guitar, played and sang—Ferrandino walked to the window and gazed on the setting sun

Ersilia would not disturb his meditations, and continued in a softer tone.

At this moment a shot was heard near the house, Ersilia, trembled violently—Lorenzo came from behind the bushes and shewed him a pheasant which he had just shot.

"A good repast for us," he said, and entered into the house.

Ferrandino went down to meet him—Upon his return he found Ersilia dancing.

"It is merely," she said, "to prevent my forgetting that which must again be my support, when I am no longer with you, dearest Ferrandino."

He laughed, and was about to reply, when Sanardo quite unexpectedly entered the chamber.

"Are you come at last," said Ferrandino.

Sanardo. Have you found the time long?

Ferrandino. How can you ask such a question?

Sanardo. Have you not a lively pleasant companion with you? She is a spaniard, and is—

Ersilia. Too modest to listen to all that you would say in her praise—

Saying this, she left the room, and ran to her hostess; singing and laughing she took upon herself for this evening the bu siness of the kitchen, to play the hostess to her guest as she said—In a short time she returned to Ferrandino's room, covered the table with wine-flasks and glasses, invited Sanardo, and again retired

Ferrandino. Now let us speak together plainly. I give you pure wine; give me the truth and conceal nothing from me.

Sanardo. Truth lies in wine.

Ferrandino. Let it be then upon your tongue also.

Sanardo. It shall be as it is upon my heart.

Ferrandino. You shewed to me a dagger too well known, and I then knew the truth of your mission—What is to be done with me? Where is the old man?

Sanardo. One question after the other —Fortunata has been taken on the island of Rosso, by a French commander, and is now closely imprisoned at Bastia—probably she will be conveyed to France. Such a woman, Pompiliani's aunt, Paoli's relation, one, who by the power of her birth, her beauty, and her eloquence may have so much influence on the hearts of her countrymen, (and has as the history of the present day demonstrates,) never will be suffered by France to remain at peace in her native land. Should she get away from there with life, yet will you never see her again. You may consider her as dead, and are the heir of her papers, and all that is in the casket, which she gave you at Cagliari, The most considerable Corsicans are scattered, and the project of placing you at the head of your brother patriots is destroyed. You well know how much you yourself have contributed to this.

Ferrandino. No reproaches?—If you had been in my place—

Sanardo. I know and feel all, that you would or could say in your defence—Enough of this!

Ferrandino. Did my friend, the old man himself, give you the dagger, which you shewed me?

Sanardo. He himself.

Ferrandino. Where is he? Where are my friends? Does Dianora live still?

Sanardo. One after the other!—It was impossible to defend you longer at Pantalaria. The blow from your friend's hand stretched you to the earth—

Ferrandino. Oh! I should have bled forth my life at Aurelia's feet!

Sanardo. Astonishment seized the soldiers. Your friend said;—" lead me to Naples; I belong to the tribunal of the king—There I shall know how to justify myself—You lay senseless at Aurelia's feet and Dianora hastened to you.

Ferrandino. O Dianora!

Sanardo. She threw herself upon your body, and kissed back your departing spirit—"He lives," she cried, and immediately you were torn bleeding from her arms by the soldiers. You were bound and brought in company with the old man to a boat, to be carried to Naples—But do you think that the wise old man had come to Pantalaria without defence?—You do not know him!—He was not alone—our band of eighty accompanied him, and Cinthio was at their head—We hastened after you. Our vessel pursued theirs, which we took; the guard was cut to pieces, and you were freed—You were taken to the island of Malta, where the old man has several good friends; you were placed in the country house of the Prince della Rocella, under the name of a relation, cured by the old man and again put in a state of happiness. Now! what say you to all this?

Ferrandino. I thank heaven that I am no longer Rinaldini.

Sanardo. You have only changed your name.

Ferrandino. My occupation also—Never will I again be seen at the head of a band of robbers—But tell me—

Sanardo. You would ask after your friends? You have perhaps already heard of the bold pirate, who is called Aladin Morad?

Ferrandino. He is said to be the terror of the Mediterranean sea—He is spoken of every where—Does any one of my friends bear this name?

Sanardo. Cinthio!

Ferrandino. Cinthio? He!—Is Cinthio, Aladin Morad?

Sanardo. He himself—All your friends who are yet in life, inhabit the little territory of the republic of Ragusa.

Ferrandino. Let us go to Ragusa.

Sanardo. Rinaldini!

Ferrandino. Call me no longer by that name.

Sanardo. Rinaldini!

Ferrandino. If you once again call me by that name, we part for ever.

Ersilia now entered the chamber, and stammered forth in terror;

" Lorenzo says that he has seen armed men in the garden."

" Armed men !" said Ferrandino, and looked inquiringly at Sanardo.

Sanardo drank off a glass of wine, and said, " I must see them—" and left the chamber.

"Have you," said Ersilia, taking Ferrandino's hand, and laying her head upon his shoulder ;—"have you any thing to fear?"

Ferrandino. What has man not to fear?

Ersilia. He has always to fear himself the most.

Ferrandino. That is true.

Ersilia. And have you to fear yourself?

Ferrandino.—Myself less than you.

Ersilia. Me ! What can you fear from me, who love you ?—But you do not hear with indifference the news of the armed men—I read it in your looks—

Ferrandino. What?

Ersilia. O Ferrandino ! Whoever you may be, do not think, that any change of your name can frighten me.

Ferrandino No.

Ersilia. Certainly not ?—No !—Not even if it were the celebrated, fearful name of———

A trampling on the steps stopped the last word on Ersilia's lips. She looked anxiously towards the door, and turned tremblingly to Ferrandino. He folded his hands, pressed them on his forhead, and stammered out—

"Am I betrayed ?"

'Gracious God ?" shrieked Ersilia, and threw her arms about his neck.

The door opened—Sanardo gave Ersilia a significant look to leave the chamber. She hesitated a while, but went.

"Have you betrayed me?" said Ferrandino, and cast a look of indignation at Sanardo.

Sanardo laughed—Ferrandino started up wildly, and cried,

"Ha? this triumphant laugh tells me my fate. I am betrayed?—but do not triumph too soon—My resolution will not let you gain so easy a victory,"

As he said this, he took a pistol, cocked it and held it to his mouth—Sanardo fell upon his arm, and the shot struck against the wall—Ersilia rushed into the chamber, Ferrandino seized the pistol, which Sanardo took from him, and turning towards the door, cried with a loud voice;

"Come in!"

"I am lost then!" exclaimed Ferrandino.

Ersilia wound her arms about him—the door opened and armed men entered the chamber—Ferrandino gazed at them with astonishment—One of the men opened his arms towards him, and shouted,

"Captain."

Ferrandino recognized the faithful Ludivico, already well known to the readers of Rinaldini.

Sanardo. Now, Sir—Am I still a traitor? Do I still laugh triumphantly?

Ferrandiño Ludivico! You!

Ludivico. Even so! Body and soul! Substantially the same.

Ferrandino. And here?

Ludovico. There is no place that I should prefer, since I am with you.

Ferrandino. I am then with friends?

Ludovico. With friends and acquaintances—Look around you!—Here are four of your former companions, who have wasted many a pound of powder under your command—They still love you—Embrace them.

He did so.

Ersilia stood at a distance, gazing in astonishment. Ludovico scarcely saw her, when he cried out;

'Ha! ha! A pretty girl too! That I could well have imagined—Still the old captain! There a guitar and here a pair of beautiful eyes—Without these he cannot live.''

Ferrandino cried out to Ersilia;

"Bring out, all that you have, Ersilia, we have dear guests, old friends and acquaintances.''

Ersilia left the room—Ludovico looked after her and said,

"By heaven she is charming!"

Ferrandino. Friends, from whence do you come?

Ludovico. From the country opposite the Italian shore.

Ferrandino. From Ragusa?

Ludovico. You have guessed rightly.

Ferrandino. Ha! I suspected as much!

Ludovico. The bold Aladin Morad, under whom we have the honour to serve has taken us a fine circuit, and lastly has brought us hither. We are now lying at anchor in the harbour, as Liparots; and are come hither as Liparots.

Ferrandino. Cinthio;

Ludovico. How! Do you then already know,—

Sanardo. He had it from me.

Ludovico. Well, then, he is on board his ship in the harbour—But here is a letter from him.

Ferrandino read the letter, while Ersilia and Madalena covered the table.—They sat down, and did not rise from the table, till the stars waxed pale in the light of the morning.

The day broke, and the whole company set out upon their journey. Their train was as numerous as the train of a little caravan.

The third day they reached Algeri, and Cinthio received his friend with open arms.

When they were in the harbour Ferrandino said to Ersilia:

"Will you go with me?"

"Yes—To the end of the world," was the answer.

They now went on board the ship, the anchor was weighed and they set sail.

Only a few stars faintly shone in the Heavens, when the waves bore the ship into the sea—And now the last stars vanished from the sky—Already the first beams of the day burst through the blue heavens. The night sunk into the west and the fleeting shadows followed it—The sky towards the east grew redder. The beams of light streamed through the pure air, and covered the blue expanse with purple streams.

Ferrandino stood upon the deck, and gazed upon the Heavens. His feeling was a silent morning prayer. Ersilia stood alone by him. Her right arm embraced him; her left hand was in his, her head rested upon his shoulder and tears stood in her eyes.

The light grew stronger, the colours became brighter—Oh! what a lovely prospect opened to their sight. A thousand golden beams of light streamed from a sin-

gle point, and spread themselves in the air.
The whole of the east seemed in flames.

Ersilia's cheeks glowed—Upon her lips
trembled the words—

"Ferrandino, do you see that?"

"I both see and feel it," he replied.

The sun now rose. Its beaming disk
hovered over the horizon—For a moment
it appeared to rest on the sea as on a
throne—and now it rose in all its clearness
and splendour, the streaming king of Heav-
en—How gloriously it rose above the water—Its glittering image was reflected a
thousand times on the surface of the waves
—And now the fiery globe seemed to stand
surrounded with a blazing light.

Ersilia was overpowered by her feelings,
as if by an electric shock—She fell upon
her knees, raised her hands and stammered;

"Glory, worthy of our prayers!"

Ferrandino sighed, and said:

"Great light of Heaven! How often
have you looked on the blood-sprinkled
plane of the robber Rinaldini! How often
have your beams pierced into my hiding-
places, unseen by mortal eyes."

Cinthio now came and said;

"Well, friend; you can no longer see
the island without a glass—It is now behind
us. So vanish the deeds in the Appen-
nines, and the mountains of Calabria?"

"Oh," sighed Ferrandino, "Oh that the remembrance could pass away with the deeds themselves."

The ship's bell rang to breakfast, and they went together into the cabin.

Sardinia already lay behind them, when a wind sprang up from the south-west—The foaming waves tossed the ship about on all sides—The night came on and the profoundest darkness enveloped them. Nothing was to be seen but the foam of the waves, that dashed so strongly against the ship, that the boldest began to fear—A thick fog gathered round them, the roaring of the wind was like the cannon's thunder. All looked anxiously for the coming day—On a sudden the vessel struck upon a rock; burst and sunk. A lamentable shriek filled the air. Ferrandino seized a broken beam.

One wave washed him into the sea, a second cast him on the shore, where weak and exhausted, he waited the approach of day.

The storm by degrees subsided—It was morning—The country became clearer—Ferrandino lay stretched beneath a tree—He looked about him, and perceived people approaching, who proved to be fishermen. They found him exhausted—He told them his misfortune, and they carried him to their huts, and gave him proper refreshment—He was told that he was on the island of Lipari—

As soon as he had in some degree recovered, they carried him to the hospital of some good-natured Bernhardin monks, who received him with kindness. He sold one of his rings, paid his good hosts, and procured clothing for himself—He had contrived to save many rings and precious stones, which for a long time secured his support, and he resolved to go into the city of the island of the same name, and take up his abode there for some time, till he had an opportunity of going to Ragusa —But it happened otherwise.

Near the monastery was a little country-house, situated in a romantic part of the country, to this place he chanced to walk one morning. He had laid himself down by a waterfall, when he heard the sound of singing, which seemed to come from a little wood close by.

The sound came nearer,—the singer came out of the bushes into the plain—Ferrandino started up, as if electrified. The moment the singer perceived him, she shrieked loudly and tremblingly supported herself against a tree,

" Poor spirit! what torments you, and

your earthly form before my eyes?"
At length she stammered with quivering
lips.

Ferrandino. I am no spirit—no spirit!
I am really here!

Female—No spirit? No vision?

Ferrandino. Neither spirit, nor vision.
I live and see you, whom I love above all,
I grasp your hand—

Female. Gracious God! Is this reality?
O, Rinaldo? Have you escaped death?

Ferrandino. I live and am thine?

As he spoke, he clasped her in his arms.
Her trembling hands were folded about his
neck; and her lips stammered

"God and the holy virgin be praised!
I have you again!—You, whom I have so
long lamented as dead!—Mine? Mine?"

"Thine! For ever thine?"

The reader will guess, whom Ferrandino
held to his breast.

With arms wound about each other,
they hastened to her dwelling, and I am
unable to paint the scene of this happy unexpected meeting.

It was Dianora, whom Ferrandino found
again.

Dianora. And you have escaped death?
My kisses recalled you to life on the
island of Dandisino, and I was bitterly re-

proached for having given you it again. You was carried away, and I remained without sensation behind. Suspecting that justice had overtaken you, and that you were publicly murdered and with ignominy, I left Pantalaria, and fled to the solitude of this silent island. Here I lamented your death, and now lament that of my faithful companion and friend, Violanta, who died a few weeks ago in my arms—I had lost every thing, and now find you again?—And all this is no dream?

Ferrandino. May it remain to us, what it is—the most delightful reality!

Dianora. This joyful moment requires witnesses.

Ferrandino. Witnesses! Is there then another person here, who knows me?

Dianora. This witness knows you not, and yet is nearly related to you.

Saying this, she left the room, but returned quickly, and brought a little child of a year old in her arms.

"My child!" cried Ferrandino, and pressed both the child and the mother with kisses to his breast.

Dianora. This is your child!—It smiles at you—It babbles the name of father!

Ferrandino. It is the voice of nature. O, wife! child!—Now am I really happy!

"Are you so?" exclaimed a voice behind him.

He turned round,—and started back in horror. Dianora sunk with a loud cry of terror on the sofa. Between them stood the black mask, already so well known to the readers of Rinaldini.

"Why," stammered Ferrandino, " Why do you thus pursue me every where?— Are you my Evil Genius? Are you a fury appointed to torment me, as once the furies followed every step of the unhappy Orestes? Though you sought me in the haunts of pillage, yet should you pass by the peaceful hut. What has the destroyer to do here? I am no longer what I was; I have trod back from the extended circle of my former activity, and live here in the narrow round of domestic life—Here is my wife! my child! They have done no evil. The child smiles innocently at the enemy of his father. Do you come for the destruction of innocence?"

„ What you are saying," replied the black, quite coolly, „ does not depend on myself."

"But my destruction depends upon you."

The mask was silent—Ferrandino continued.

„ In me you murder a husband and a

father! Are not these names holy with you?"

"The commands of my superiors, are alone holy with me."

"And they desire my death?"

The mask answered the question in the affirmative, by bowing his head.

"Then murder me here before the eyes of my wife and child—But you must murder me, and I will sell my life dear—You are the first that falls."

With this he took a pair of pistols from the wall, and placed himself between the mask and the door.

"What are you about?" exclaimed the mask, in evident confusion.

"I fight for existence—If you seek again the robber-chief in me, you shall find him. You know that Rinaldini could fight; you shall also learn, that Ferrandine can fight as well."

"What would you do?"

"At the first appearance of violence against me, you lie dead at my feet.'

"Will that protect you?"

"If it will not protect me, it will at least avenge me."

"Hear me!—Those, whom you fear, have founded for the advantage of the state a secret tribunal, and stand under the no preme command of the Inquisition. When we first knew you, our intentions towards you were good and for your advantage. You were obstinate and would not listen to us. That old impostor pierced your breast at Pantalaria—This woman's kisses recalled you into life. You were brought to the ship, and your companions murdered the royal guard. One only escaped, who saved his life by swimming to Pantalaria. I went back to Sicily and lived there quietly—Eight days ago my superiors sent me hither on business. I saw you here with the same astonishment that you saw me—I will pretend not to have seen you; I will demand no assistance against you —But what will you give me? and how will you reward my silence?"

"You shall not escape me," said Ferrandino. "These smooth words only spring from your necessity. You go, and I shall be arrested. Your only object now is to escape this ball, but that cannot be. Prudence compels me to one murder—God forgive me! I murder one sinner for my own security—It cannot be otherwise. I defend myself, my wife, my child! God be merciful to you!"

He cocked the pistol, and the mask fell down on his knees before him.

"But one word! he exclaimed, with folded hands.

"What have you got to say?"

"Let me pray, and murder me in prayer."

Ferrandino retreated a few steps. The mask got up slowly, looked up to Heaven and pointed to the child. Ferrandino turned round and looked at the boy. At this moment the Black sprang forward, darted towards him, pressed him with his well known strength and threw him to the ground. The pistol went off, the ball struck the ceiling, and Ferrandino cried with stifled voice;

"I am lost!"

Dianora sprang from the sofa, wild and raging like a Lioness. She drew a dagger from his breast, and plunged it with all the strength of despair into the Black's throat, —He groaned heavily and died.

"You are saved!" cried Dianora, joyfully.

Ferrandino pressed her to his breast.

"Whither, oh whither, shall we go, Dianora?" he exclaimed.

Dianora. Wheresoever you go, there will Dianora. I, your wife, the mother of this child, and for your sake a monsteress, follow you throughout the world,

Ferrandino. O Dianora! What a dreadful misfortune has embittered the enjoyments of our happiness!

Dianora. That it should have been so!

Ferrandino. I am an ill-starred man!

Dianora. And before you thought yourself happy.

Ferrandino. But see! Here lies bathed in blood the fearful pledge of our misfortune.

Dianora left the room, went out of the house, and looked around, but saw nobody. She came back.

"The deed," she said, "has been done without any witnesses but ourselves—Who then will accuse us of it? My maid is in the fields, and the child's nurse is still in the city, whither I sent her: Let us now conceal our victim."

It was done, and towards midnight Ferrandino carried the body to the shore, and committed it to the waves.

It was impossible for them to remain any longer in Lipari. Dianora preferred the old concealed castle in Sicily as the place of their future abode; but Ferrandino did not think it advisable to go to Sicily, and after much debate they concluded to visit their friends at Ragusa.

For this purpose they hired a passage-boat, and set sail with a favorable wind.

They had been but a few hours at sea, when an armed bark came up with them which overpowered their vessel, and took it back to Lipari, in the name of the Viceroy, as the captain said.

They disembarked, and towards evening were carried to the city. Dianora, the child, and the maid, were led to the convent of the Ursulines, and Ferrandino was brought to a state prison in the castle.

Here he remained two days; early in the morning of the third he was taken before the Viceroy.

He was brought into a room, where the viceroy was not present. A government secretary heard his deposition, and took it down in writing.

" Your name ?"

" Ferrandino "

" Where born ?"

" At Rome."

" You are not a Corsican, then ?"

" No !"

" On your oath, not ?"

" On my oath, I am not."

" You were in Sardinia ?"

" Two months."

" Your acquaintance ?"

" They were such as a stranger and a traveller could find."

"Did you not know any Corsicans, when in Sardinia?"

"Two ladies, whom I first learnt to be Corsicans, when they were arrested."

"How did you leave Sardinia?"

"In a Ragusan vessel. I was shipwrecked upon this island; my companions have probably perished."

"Why did you not announce yourself to the governor of Lipari?"

"I was with the Bernhardine monks, and supposed they would know what was right for me or them to do."

"How did you meet with that lady, in whose company you were brought here?"

"She is an acquaintance of mine."

"An acquaintance!"

"My wife, whom I have found miraculously after a long seperation."

"Why did you leave the island without a passport?"

"Whither are you going?"

"To Ragusa."

"Have you relations there?"

"Acquaintances and friends."

"Foreigners or countrymen?"

"Foreigners, who have settled there."

"Did you sell her this ring, which I shew you?"

"Yes, I gave it to the Bernhardines and

sold it to pay my reckoning, and to provide clothes for myself."

"Where did you get this ring?"

"I bought it long ago of a Florentine jew."

"The ring has been stolen."

"I did not know that."

"Sign the Protocol."

Ferrandino signed the Protolcol, and the secretary sent it up to the viceroy.

The servant who took it up, soon returned, and brought back orders that he should follow him to the viceroy—Ferrandino followed.

The viceroy sat at a writing table, and turned round to him, as the servant left the chamber. He looked at him, and the Protocol dropped from his hands.—Ferrandino drew back in terror, and pressing his folded hands upon his forehead threw himself at the viceroy's feet.

Ferrandino. O my prince!

Viceroy. Man! Do I again see you!—Why did you not stay at Malta? O Ferrandino, as you now call yourself—Ferrandino! Do you dare venture again into the states of the king of Sicily? How much your presence confounds me! I know who you are, I am here to represent the king, and my duty commands me to do that, which my friendship for you can scarcely prevent me from doing without injustice.

Ferrandino. I am in your power—I do not entreat for myself, but for my wife—my child—

Viceroy. Your wife?

Ferrandino. Dianora! the unhappy Dianora. The Prince della Rocella, was always noble minded, and now—

Viceroy. My fortune vexes me through you—Go back to your prison,—I will see what can be done for you—this ring was once mine—In your hands it was—

Ferrandino. You know—

Viceroy. I will buy it again.

Ferrandino. Lives— dare I ask the question?—

Viceroy. I guess what you would ask

Ferrandino. Does Aurelia live still

Viceroy. She still lives.

Ferrandino. She still lives?—Here;—With you?

Viceroy. She will receive Dianora as a sister.

Ferrandino. She is—

Viceroy. She is the Abbess of the Ursulines with whom Dianora now is—Enough for the present—Your appearance has disturbed me—I need repose.

Ferrandino kissed his hand in tears, and was reconducted to the castle.

For ten days he lay in the solitude of his prison, and nobody seemed to lament his fate. He wrote letters to the Viceroy, to Dianora, and to Aurelia, but he waited in vain for an answer—At length he received a note from the Viceroy—He opened it hastily and read—

"After many conflicts between duty and benevolence, I can resolve upon nothing but to alleviate your fate. You will however feel that even by this I have done much for you—Consider and decide—this evening you will see me."

In the evening he was led to the prince. He thanked him for his kindness, and the prince replied with emotion ;

"I neither can nor dare do more for you, than I have done already, and—am now about to do. You will be conducted to-night to the harbour, and be taken on board an English frigate. It is going to Ragusa, and will carry you to your friends."

"How shall I, how can I sufficiently thank you for this magnanimity ?"

The Prince. I expect no thanks—May you be happy.—You have written to Aurelia; she sends you her best wishes, and would, but may not, speak to you.

Ferrandino. And Dianora?

The Prince. She cannot go with you!

Ferrandino. How !

The Prince. She remains here !

Ferrandino. Can she do so ?—Is it her own will ?

The Prince. She must for her own sake and that of her child.

Ferrandino. Prince !

The Prince, Let me not say to you, what you may say to yourself—The Countess Martyno remains here. She has her possessions in Sicily, she is—Enough— Besides she is now ill.

Ferrandino. Ill ?

The Prince. Very ill !—Her senses are disturbed—She laments a murder that she has committed.

Ferrandino. A Murder ?

The Prince. She cannot be in her senses. You know in what a state she was once before ; she is weak, her health is shaken, her nerves are overstretched. She remains here.

Ferrandino. O Dianora ! I must then leave you, lose you, because I have found you again—And my child—

The Prince. He shall be mine. What education, what pretensions to fortune and success in the world can *you* give him?— *You,* who are a man despised and pursued, whose real name is already become a crime?

Ferrandino. Gracious Heavens!

The Prince. I will free the child from this blot—I will openly declare him to be my own.

Ferrandino. Prince!

The Prince. I shall thus give him a name unsullied by guilt, and preserve for him the property of his mother. He will then grow up, and live in esteem and never know who was his father.

Ferrandino. Dreadful fate! Oh my son, my son! Where will thy father find the end of his laborious wretched pilgrimage?

The Prince. Let him see your grave without blushing, and he may yet be happy.

Ferrandino. Oh God! May it be so, dear, unfortunate child! And you, beloved Dianora! alas, you—

The Prince. I see her in the dress of the Ursulines quietly meet death, as—my unhappy child.

Ferrandino. Prince! These tears—

The Prince. You have already given two Ursulines to the church, to themselves and to repose—And what will you do?

Ferrandino. There are Carthusian cells.

The Prince. MEMENTO MORI.

Ferrandino. I will—

The Prince. You are going to Ragusa— You will there find acquaintances, friends, the *old man of Fronteia*. They certainly do not live together in quiet; they are employed in some plan; you will take a part in it—

Ferrandino. No!

The Prince. Whatsoever you do, return not to Italy, return not to Sicily

Ferrandino. Oh, why did Dianora's kisses recall me to life?

The Prince. It has happened so!—Our knowledge, actions, wishes, strength, are human. A higher power watches over us, which we cannot resist—What it has resolved must happen—Go—Worship your Creator; become a good man, and resign yourself quietly to the guidance of the rulers of the world. God be with you! His holy angel accompany you. Travel in happiness!

As he said this, he pressed a passport into his hand, wiped the tears from his eyes, and left the room. Ferrandino looked after him, and sobbed violently. He was now carried off, and brought into the harbour. At break of day, he went on board the vessel, and the sun rose above the horizon, when they put to sea.

"O Dionora! O my son!" he exclaimed, "these rolling waves bear me from you and I shall never see you again. The poor labourer can rest on the bosom of his wife; bound round with the bonds of conjubial love and joy, he forgets himself, his misfortunes and the world. But I unhappy! must see my wife fly to the reffuge of a cloister, must beg from my friends another name for my child, that he may not see his sorrow.

"O my wife! my son! May God grant you in a two-fold proportion that rest and happiness, which is denied to your unhappy father who gave you life, and whom you may not thank for the gift—when the name of your father is mentioned, you like the rest of mankind, will not be able to conceal your abhorrence, and will not know that it is your father that you abhor. Gracious Heaven! grant to my son your grace let him become a good man and in him I shall have given that to the world, which I did not give to it in myself. To the fire with the tree, which has borne such evil fruit—let another take its place—I yield to my son."

"Sir," said the captain, "I have received orders from the Viceroy to give you this casket, when we were at sea. Here it is."

Ferrandino took the casket, opened it in the cabin, and found a considerable sum of money for his travelling expences.

"Alas!" he sighed, "good man, you can indeed give me gold, but who can give me that which I so much need—Who can give me rest?"

He heard a loud sighing in the adjoining chamber.

He trembled in terror—but again collecting himself approached the partition. He looked through a chink, and saw a woman sitting at a table, her head leaning upon her hand, and her eyes covered with a handkerchief; she seemed to be weeping or in thought.

"Who is here besides myself unhappy?" said Ferrandino.

"I," said the female, and started up.

Ferrandino saw her, and hastened out of his cabin into hers.

"Fiametta!" he exclaimed. "May I trust my eyes? Is it really you?"

"Ferrandino! How—here?"

"What a strange accident!"

He looked round the room as if in search of something.

Fiammetta laughed, and said;

"I gess what you are looking for.'

Ferrandino. Is Fortunata here?

Fiammeta. No!

Ferrandino. Where is she?

Fiammetta. She is now probably far advanced on her way to France, or perhaps is confined in a cloister at Bastia.

Ferrandino.   And you?

Fiammetta.   By artifice and the exertions of a friend I have escaped.   Now will I go upon an adventure to Sicily; perhaps I may find some service at Messina or Palermo.

Ferrandino.   Service!

Fiammetta.   What else?

Ferrandino.   So beautiful a woman.

Fiammetta.   I know many more beautiful women, who are yet in service.

Ferrandino.   Fortune is unjust.

Fiammetta.   Was it ever otherwise?

Ferrandino   You must not serve.

Fiammetta.   Can you shew me any other mode by which I may gain an honourable subsistence?

Ferrandino.   Will you go with me?

Fiammetta.   Whither?

Ferrandino.   To Ragusa.

Fiammetta.   And what should I do there?

Ferrandino.   I—I will bring you as a companion to a female friend.

Fiammetta.   Are the Corsicans safe at Ragusa?

Ferrandino.   Were you then engaged in a plot with them?

Fiammetta,   A *plot*? None of the family of Pompitiani, or Paloi enter into *plots*, but they would venture all, even *life*, to free their country from the chains with which injustice and pride have fettered it.—— I am a woman, a weak creature, but could I free my country, I would not regard my life, my blood, nor even my freedom. I would die in chains, in the most horrible dungeon, could I but say; *Corsica is free.*

Ferrandino. Are you also of Paoli?

Fiammetta. Pondarini. The name of my ancestor is well known. He fought for the freedom of his country, and often with Theodore.—He fell for the freedom of the Corsicans, I am an orphan and without a friend.

Ferrandino And Ferrandino lives still.

Fiammetta. O Fortunata.

Ferrandino. She is not here.

Fiammetta. If she knew——

Ferrandino. That Ferrandino remembers her, she would then——

At this moment Fortunata entered the room.

Ferrandino shrunk back in astonishment and exclaimed.

"Am I always to be the sport of women,?"

"Not the sport of women, but of your own passions."

"Adieu," said Fiammetta, and left the chamber.

'O Fortunata, if you knew——"

"What?"

'Hear me."

He then related the history of Dianora, and of his being forced to leave her and his child.

Fortunata. And why did you leave them?

Ferrandino. My fate compelled me.

Fortunata. Who are you?

Ferrandino. As a proof that I love you, I give up my name. I am——

Fiammetta returned at this critical moment, and asked if they were reconciled.

"We are," said Fortunata and threw herself into his arms.

BOOK III.

Fiammetta had prevented Ferrandino from discovering his secret and in the interval he had time for reflection. Fortunata, although tortured by curiosity, remained silent, and asked no more, as she perceived that he wished to evade the subject. In this manner passed away several tedious days.

A calm caused him wearisome days and tedious hours. Fortunata related her history, and initiated Ferrandino in the secrets of her birth and fate. She set a value on the confidence, and gave him to understand that one confidence deserved another.

"It does so!"—said Ferrandino, composedly; "but it will be better for us both if Fortunata never learns who he is, whom she has entrusted with her confidence and to whom she has given what is much more; *to whom she has given* her love."

She looked at him smilingly, sunk her eyes on the ground and slowly said :

" That I have done !"

Ferrandino silently imprinted a kiss on her forehead and percieved tears in her eyes. Surprised, he asked her :

"What is that ?"

She dried her eyes, and was about to speak, when Fiammetta approached them. She took his hand and asked :

"Where are we really going ? to Sicily or to Ragusa ?"

" To Ragusa ;" replied Ferrandino.

" Have you already settled upon it ?", continued Fiammetta—

Both paused.

Fiammetta. Now ? What is that ?—I mean you have agreed about. Have you not ?

Fortunata. It has not been mentioned.

Fiammetta. Then let it be now.—To-morrow the Captain anchors at Palermo, and we must either disembark or proceed further.

Ferrandino. We will disembark.

Fiammetta. Really ? What ! have you been quarrelling ?

Fortunata. Who should quarrel ?

Fiammetta. You are rufled. That you cannot deny.—What has been the matter?

Fortunata. Between us there is nothing but secrets.

Ferrandino. It is not always prudent to endeavour to unravel secrets. Sometimes we find more, sometimes less than we hope to find. But a secret is unfolded.

Fortunata. Mine.

Ferrandino. That the ladies will not accompany me to Ragusa, that they will remain in Sicily. Sicily is a fine, fruitful, pleasant and excellent country.

Fortunata. Have you been in Sicily ?

Fiammetta. Have you any friends there?

Ferrandino. I had a friend in Sicily, whom I loved more than myself.

Fortunata. That's saying much ;—for you are a strong egotist.

The Captain approached and announced that he should anchor to-morrow at Palermo, and that he should remain there three days.

" There continued he, "we shall have much pleasure, and find all joyful for the feast of the holy Rosalie, the *Protecting Patroness* of the place, is kept on that day, and on that occasion there is much mirth and pleasantry."

The Captain mentioned the holy Rosalie

and Ferrandino thought of the terrestrial angel of that name, whom he knew so well.

"Rosalie!" exclaimed he.

"Yes; Rosalia she is called; the holy Rosalie," she may have been a good girl and a little more decent than a certain Rosalia who shines in all the Sicilian ballads which are sung of Rinaldini.

Ferrandino. He is dead.

Captain. Long ago.

Ferrandino. Did you know him?

Captain, God forbid! with that sort of men I have no connection.

Ferrandino. I knew him.

Captain. Indeed! Were you ever in his clutches?

Ferrandino. Fast.

Captain. And I suppose he pulled you about finely.

Ferrandino. He did, indeed.

Captain. . There I will believe you without swearing. It is said he was a crafty impostor.

Ferrandino had reasons for breaking off the discourse, and when he was alone with his peevish companion, he seized her hand and said,—

"Fortunata! the secret which I would have discovered to you, would perhaps make you my enemy: remain what you me, my friend. There are years of my life on which I look back with reluctancy. Excuse a recollection that is unpleasant and painful to me. You can lose nothing by it. But if you insist on your request, I will gratify it, yet that cannot be done before we reach Ragusa."

" You have heard," said Fortunata, composedly, "that we shall remain in Sicily."

Ferrandino entreated her to accompany him to Ragusa: she kept to her original resolution, and for the present every thing remained undetermined.

Night wore apace and with day-break they were at anchor before Palermo.

All was in a joyful uproar———She lives! the holy Rosalie lives! echoed from all the streets, which were planted with trees, strewed with flowers, and hung with tapestry. Music and loud huzzas, welcomed the arrival of the strangers, and those who could leave the ship, hurried into the town, to participate in the joyful festival. Fortunata and Fiammetta did so, but Ferrandino remained in the ship. It appeared singular to the Captain, and it occurred to him that his passenger was unwell or an eccentric, and deserved to be an Englishman.

Towards evening the ladies returned to

the ship. They entertained themselves with conversing upon the solemnities they witnessed, and spoke of lodgings which were to be let.—Ferrandino was silent.

The following morning the ladies went again into the city, and Ferrandino remained, as before, in the ship.

When Fortunata and Fiammetta returned towards evening, they were less affable than the day before.—They found Ferrandino absorbed in deep meditation, and Fortunata approached him.

Fortunata. Ferrandino has either singular humours or very weighty reasons, that withhold him from being present at the solemnities of Palermo.

Fiammetta. perhaps the former more than the latter.

Fortunata. Is it painful reccollections that deter you from entering the city?

Ferrandino. It is.

Fiammetta. Palermo is a gay, interesting place, and we shall have much pleasure there.

Ferrandino. Do you really intend to remain at Palermo?

Fiammetta. Well now! we will try.

Ferrandino. You will not go with me to Ragusa?

Fortunata. Upon what footing shall we live with you among your relations?

Ferrandino. As the friends of me and my acquaintances.

In the ship was heard a loud shout and a wild huzza! The sailors were hailing their Captain, who in company with other drunken companions, and a band of musicians, returned from the city. Ferrandino very distinctly heard them cry:

"Long life to the Ragusians!"

Ferrandino at this outcry left the cabin. The ship was illuminated, and the deck crowded with joyful men.

The Captain saw him and called out to him:

"Now, hypocondriac! will you too see how it goes where there are jovial men?" and handed him a brimming goblet.

Ferrandino drank, and asked after the Ragusian.

"There he stands," replied the Captain, "he is a pleasant fellow, and our ship-neighbour."

He went up to him, and the Ragusian started back. Ferrandino gave significant winks and looks, and hurried back to his cabin, whither the Ragusian followed him. The ladies had retired to their cabin.

Ferrandino. Luigino? is it possible? Are you really himself?

Luigino. Let me return you the same question

Ferrandino. Where do you come from?

Luigino. I come from Ragusa, go by the name of Grandamore, and am Captain of the frigate Olympia. I am in search of a certain Aladdin Morad, alias Cinthio.

Ferrandino. Alas? his grave you will never find.

Luigino. What do you say?

Ferrandino. In his ship, with him, I left Sardinia. The ship was wrecked in a storm on the rocks of Lipari, and I unfortunate was the only one that escaped the dreadful wreck.

Luigino. Poor Cinthio! poor friends who with him were buried in the deep. We guessed that some misfortune had happened to him, but that he was dead———. Friend! in him we lose much!———and you escaped?

Ferrandino. A wave, which should have swallowed me, threw me contemptuously on the shore.

Luigino. And that you take to be wonderful!

Ferrandino. What more shall I do in this world?

Luigino. Live and effect.

Ferrandino. What?

Luigino. You are still the same.

Ferrandino. That would not be very acceptable to God.

Luigino. Always so solemn. But yet you are on the way to Ragusa?

Ferrandino. Yes; I am going there.

Luigino. Then my ship will be turned round and conduct you to your expecting friends. To-morrow you go on board my ship, and respecting this business we will not say another word to-day.

Fortunata and Fiammetta separated from them only by a wooden partition, had heard distinctly the whole of this discourse; but how much to guess and to conjecture was left to their curiosity. They slept little, but Ferrandino still less.

At breakfast Ferrandino requested them to give him a decided declaration, and received it. Both persisted in remaining at Palermo.

"At least for the present," added Fiammetta, "but if it does not please us in Palermo, Messina, or any where else, we will come, with your permission, to Ragusa and search you out."

As the ladies were going into the city, the parting scene was instantly solemnized. It was not without tears. The ladies went. Ferrandino left Fortunata some jewels, put a tender billet with them, sealed them up, and laid them on the table in her cabin, went on board a boat, arrived at the Ragusian ship, entered, and was received by Luigino with open arms.

They already descried Sicilians in chase of them and made towards the Island of Pantalaria. Ferrandino hung with melancholy looks on the island. With the telescope he thought he could discover his former-habitation. He saw the lonely cross-chapel, called to mind the sweet scenes of the past, thought on Dianora and his son, and tears rolled down his cheeks.

"It is all gone by," said he, "it passed away like a fleeting shadow and even the remembrance itself leaves an impression but like that of a vision. I hasten towards new scenes yet know not how they will please me."

Pantalaria vanished from his sight, his sighs evaporated in the air, and his ardent gaze was lost in the boundless ocean.

They swept by Limosa and Lampidosa, and after a short but favourable voyage, arrived at the place of their destination, anchored in the harbour of Ragusa and disembarked.

"Three miles from the city," said Luigino, "the Old Man inhabits an elegant villa, there we will surprise him. As yet he knows nothing of our arrival, and I promise myself a grand feast on this surprisal.

They took horses and set out for the villa, which they reached towards evening. They alighted and went through the garden towards the house.—Ferrandino's heart throbbed violently.

They saw a large richly covered table set out in the open air, which they had scarce approached, when a boy came towards them and said,—

"The Old Man of Fronteia welcomes his dear guests, and greets the noble Ferrandino."

"Does he know that I am here?" asked Ferrandino.

"He does," replied the boy.

They looked at each other in silence and with surprise. Luigino shook his head.

"The Old Man is still the same," said Ferrandino, and went further.

A girl then flew from a bush towards him, threw her arms around his neck, kissed him, and cried:

"Are you with us too at last?"

The girl was Serena. Ferrandino returned her kisses, but not without confusion, and asked:—

"Are you here too' Serena?"

"As you see; and my wishes to see you again, are fulfilled.'

A soft agreeable music sounded from an

adjacent hedge, and the wise Old Man of
Fronteia came towards them, clad in a sky-
blue Grecian habit; a purple cloak was
slung round his shoulders, a wreath of lau-
rels encircled his temples.   He approached
Ferrandino with a friendly look, presented
his left hand to him, and said:

"Welcome to me and to all your friends!
With friendship I present you the hand of
salutation and of a joyful reception.   It is
the left, it is the hand nearest to the heart.
It is the left which even out of friendship
never lifts a dagger against an enemy; and
the right may know what the left does. .
But it is not so in the reversed case.
Once more I bid you welcome! you were
at a distance, but your heart was always
with us, and the hearts of your friends were
with you.   Now they are again together,
embrace me, brave Ferrandino, and salute
your friends."

He embraced him and Olympia came towards them.   She opened her arms, and
Ferrandino clasped her to his bosom.

"Then I see you again?" stammered
Ferrandino.

"You see us again?" said the Old Man,
"and we rejoice at your wished for return,
here in the lap of peace and content." .

The others pressed towards them, and

the scene of welcome became general. Serena lisped to Ferrandino

"I was the first who met you!"

He nodded to her, and squeezed her hand tenderly, which she returned with ardour.

"Now to table," said the Old Man, who seated himself at the head, and Ferandino took place at his left hand. Serena sat near him, and Olympia sat at the right of the wise Old Man.

The heavens were serene, the evening freshness mild, and the breeze so pure and gentle as scarce to agitate the flames of twenty large wax candles which were burning on the table. The reflecting rays of light illumined the arbour in various different ways, alternately producing light and dark shades on the foliage. Here some leaves were of a shining yellow, while others were obscured in a dark green. Here glittered the white blossom hanging from long winding stalks on the gold-yellow earth; there two upright leaves permitting the rays of a star to enter sparkled like a diamond. The cool night air held the rooty exhalations of the flowers prisoner in the earth and gave them two-fold refreshment. The fluttering reflection which played on the light and shade of the foliage—all this gave an inexpressible charm to the table-scene.

The Old Man took a tankard, poured wine into a golden shell, and drank with these words,—

"To those of our friends who found their grave in the deep!"

They all repeated this and followed his example.

Ferrandino added,—

"To thee, my Cinthio! to thee, brave Ludovico! and thee, good Ersilia!"

Olympia smiled, seized her goblet, inclined it towards Ferrandino and said:

"To your good Ersilia!"

"To your dear friend!"—added Serena, and sounded her goblet against Ferrandino's.

"To all good souls!"—said Luigino; and his health became general.

"You are among friends Ferrandino! began the Old Man;—among friends, who know and' esteem you. Relate to them your adventures."

Ferrandino related them, universal attention engrossed the hearers. When he came to the departure from the prince and the leaving of his son behind, tears started from his eyes, he covered his face and could not proceed

There arose a deep pause. The Old Man made a sign, and the music interrupted it. An universal chorus resounded.

The singing and music grew silent.—The old Old Man said considerately,

" Ferrandino ! proceed in your narration."

He did so, and when he had ended, the Old Man seized his hand, and said :

Friend ! you are come to friends —The present obscures the past.—The storm passes over and genial sunbeams calm the trembling heart. Man is born for the world. He must conform himself to the times. Joy should not make him presumptuous. Misfortunes should never make him dejected. Night follows day. The Aurora and the red of Even, glitter in the same horrizon.

Serena rose up, took a garland formed of fragrant roses, twined it with trembling hand in the locks of Ferrandino, and with a sweet voice, accompained by tunes and harps and flutes, sang :

Ferrandino imprinted a kiss on her glowing cheeks, and the Old Man said :

" It is the gift of joy, which a tender heart presents you."

" I know how to value both ;"—returned Ferrandino.

" And in doing so that you do well!"— added Olympia.

The others at the table gradually became noisy, made themselves remarkable, and were severally presented to his guests by name, and recommended them as friends. Ferrandino ran over all their countenances superficially, but on one he remained firmly fixed. The beauty to whom this interesting countenance belonged, was called by the Old Man, without further remarks, Serafina.

Ferrandino, already pretty well heated with wine, seized his goblet and said,—

" Beauteous Serafina ! while I entreat your friendship, I give you the assurance of mine."

Blushing the lovely damsel replied :

' I receive your agreeable gift with pleasure, and beg to remain always in possession of it, as I shall endeavour to deserve it."

Olympia. Our friend Serafina thinks and feels delicately, and Ferrandino may rely on the assurance she gives here.

Serena. She has already before she knew you, interested herself very much for you.

Serafina. As all the friends of Ferrandino have done. I have only followed the universal sentiment.

Ferrandino. I beg you will preserve it Presence not seldom destroys the edifice of expectation as quick as it was raised,

Serafina. What I have once erected, I do not willingly destroy. It usually remains although useless.

Olympia. That is the character of constancy.—Can Ferrandino boast of that too?

Ferrandino. I believe so.

Olympia. Well then, I believe it to!

A boy brought the Old Man letters. He read them very attentively, thrust them into his bosom, and appeared to be more serene than he had been.—Olympia remarked it. She smiled at him kindly. He nodded to her as kindly. She took a golden shell and said,—

"When joy makes cheerful men happy, they should always think on the unfortunate, and where merry-making reigns poverty finds benevolent friends!"

She threw money in the shell. All followed her example. She emptied the shell, beckoned to a boy, gave him the money and said,—

"The poor woman in the forest!"

'Generous, compassionate benefactress,' said the Old Man; "you have acted most charitably."

Soon after the Old Man rose from his

seat, spoke a few words, and the table was removed. In a long line, two and two, the company followed the Old Man, who with Olympia went before and entered the house.

The company dispersed themselves, and many strolled about the garden.

Ferrandino went towards a waterfall, and threw himself down in an orange-arbour near it.

He had not lain here long when rustling footsteps interrupted him in his contemplation. They came nearer, and Serafina stood before him. She appeared to be confused and stammered:

'I did not expect you to have been here You repose on my favourite spot !"

"Then permit me to share it with you," replied Ferrandino; seized her hand and gently drew her down to him.

" You was, it appeared, absorbed in deep meditation. If I should disturb you———."

" I was employed with Serafina."

" With me ? How could I———."

" Furnish me with a subject for employment ? Serafina might ask."

" You are, as I have always heard you reported, very gallant."

" Yet more than that ; I am always sincere."

Serafina was silent   Ferrandino seized her hand, and played with her fingers. He sighed.—Sighing, she became the echo of these sighs. He seized her other hand. Their glowing cheeks approached each other; their lips met in silence. In the loud rustling of the waterfall their interchanged kisses sounded but softly. The moon-beams shone clearly on the surface of the water, and peeped through the arbour. Here played eyes in eyes, here reposed, with long respiration, lips on lips, and arms were twined with arms. Ferrandino's lips sunk lower, and an elastic bosom heaved towards his soft glowing kisses, and struggling they endeavoured to clasp each other in their arms.

"Ferrandino!" cried a voice at a little distance.

Serafina suddenly started up, and trembling, hurried out of the arbour. Ferrandino went, chagrined, towards the waterfall, from whence the voice proceeded.

Here stood a boy who said,—

"I have been looking for you to show you your chamber. Our master is already gone to rest and wishes you a good night."

Ill-humouredly Ferrandino followed the boy into the house, and was conducted across a gallery to an elegant chamber. In a second chamber he saw his couch. Wine and fruit stood on the table, on which lay also a guitar.

As he had nothing more to command, the boy left him. But he went out of the chamber, up and down the gallery with violent steps, and passed many chamber doors.

He had not long paced up and down, when a light shone opposite to him, and some one came towards him. It was Olympia. A boy preceded her with a wax light, and she was led by a young man. They looked at each other, and smiled. Olympia wished him a good night, and, pointing to a chamber-door, they disappeared.

"What can she mean?" said he to himself. "Perhaps in this chamber—What —? If Serafina—?"

Quickly determined, he knocked, opened the door, and entered a chamber faintly illuminated. He hastily entered, and as hastily left it.—Six skeletons sat at a table in the chamber. He saw no further; shut the door, and was hurrying to his chamber, when the door of the so dreadfully decorated apartment, which he had just left, opened, and a voice softly called to him, "Ferrandino."

Confounded he looked back, and perceived Serafina.

"What do you do among the dead?" he hastily asked.

She made signs to him to be silent. With irresolute step he went towards her, seized her hand, and said,—

"I wished to see, to speak to you, adored Serafina! and saw———.'

She again made signs to him to be silent, and whispered:

"Follow me."

With that she seized his hand, and led him into the chamber in which the skeletons were sitting at the table, they passed through that, and through a second into her apartment. Here she threw her arms around his neck, and kissed him and said,—

"Think not ill of me! I only lead you to explanations."

Ferrandino. To explations? First let me request explanation.

Serafina. Which?

Ferrandino. What means your being with skeletons?

Serafina. I do not know.

Ferrandino. What do you do here among such monsters?

Serfiana. Duty obliges me thereto for this night.

Ferrandino. Duty ! and only for this night ? Explain yourself more distinctly.

Serafina. But this I can tell you, that all of us who live here in this palace with the Old Man are bound by duty, when it is our turn, to pass the night in this chamber and to take care that the lamp which hangs above the skeletons is not extinguished. To-night the watch is on me.

Ferrandino Strange !—How often does it fall to your turn ?

Serafina. Scarcely three times in the year

Ferrandino. And are you not afraid ?

Serafina. What should I fear ? These skeletons ? I fear you more !

Ferrandino. Me ?

Serafina. You.

Ferrandino. Oh, Serafina ! how can you fear what loves you ?

Serafina. Loves !—But how do you love me ?

Ferrandino. As my life.

Serafina. Reflect on what you say and promise.

Ferrandino. That I have done long ago.

Serafina. Done ?—No ! consider, and speak of it another time with me. You are free ; so am I. Do you really love me ?—Nothing shall oppose our union But without priestly benediction——

A bell just then tolled.

Ferrandino. What is that?

Serafina. Go Ferandino! That is the toll of the hour of midnight. You must now leave me. I must be alone, and no man dare, on pain of heavy punishment, be found with me. So it is willed by our commandment.

He looked at her, and quickly left the chamber.

In the gallery he took breath, and was just going into his chamber, when a door near it opened, from which Serena came towards him. She stretched out her hand after his. He gave it her, and willingly suffered her to draw him into her chamber.

Serena. Is Ferandino become a night-walker?

Ferrandino. I have been creeping about the gallery a long while looking for your chamber.

Serena. Only my chamber? Why not myself? Or do you change the names ?— Would you not say Serafina?

Ferrandino. Serena sounds much more pleasing

Serena. That you can bring in verse. In prose I tell you that you are not to be trusted, and that I have noticed every look which you gave Serafina across the table.

Ferrandino. She is interesting.

Serena. There we have it.

Ferrandino. But nevertheless no Serafina.

Serena. I appeal to the truth.

Ferrandino. It throws itself in your arms!

With that he embraced and kissed her heartily.—Smiling she disengaged herself, and threw herself, loudly laughing, on a sofa.

Ferrandino. At what do you laugh so immoderately?

Serena. To think that Serafina is sitting by skeletons, while I have it in my power to make her lover faithless.

Ferrandino. Will you do that?

Serena. Why not?

Ferrandino. But you do not trust me.

Serena. What matters that? I cannot desire that you should love me better than you have loved the dearest of your mistresses, Aurelia, Rosalia, Olympia, Dianora, Ersilie, and who knows how many more, as you would and will love, even Serafina. You love very inconstantly. Like as the moon loves the earth, sometimes not at all, generally half, and only on a few days with full adhesion. That I know. But what shall one do when one is good to you? One must be contented. You cannot give more than you have. Faithful love is a prohibited coin with you, which you never carry What you have and give can be immediately exchanged, and at premium your coins stand as little as your capital at interest. Let us for once see how long we shall love one another and who will deceive the other first ! But that must be done after a manner. Not true.—How much will you bet that I do not fix you for to-day?

He clasped her, smiling, in his arms; she threw her arms around his neck.—In this manner they saluted Aurora and the golden morning sun.

Ferrandino had not long returned to his chamber, when Olympia invited him to a morning walk in the garden. He went there and found her in a pavilion.

'Now, my noble friend." said she, to him, smiling, " have you been well entertained by the living among the dead ?"

Ferrandino. I dared not disturb the watch.

Olympia. Aha !

Ferrandino. Why are these figures watched, which will certainly not run away ?

Olympia. It is an order of the Old Man.

Ferrandino. Who were these skeletons formerly ?

Olympia. Their names stand on their skulls. Read them there yourself.

After a pause, during which breakfast was brought in, when the servants were at a distance, the discourse recommenced.

Ferrandino. I am now with you.—For what can you or will you use me!

Olympia. That will shew itself.

Ferrandino. The Old Man lives here on a *smooth* footing.

Olympia. Quiet and unnoticed, as we believe.

Ferrandino. He entertains many guests.

Olympia. As he has always done.

Ferrandino. So then he is rich?

Olympia. Certainly.

Ferrandino. Olympia!—Shall we be sincere to one another?

Olympia. To the best of my knowledge I have always been so.

Ferrandino. Accepted! Then you will be so now!

Olympia. I will.

Ferrandino. Can you reveal a secret to me?

Olympia. What?

Ferrandino. Who is the Old Man?

Olympia. Friend!—That I do not know But if I dare trust my conjectures, he is— yet, between you and I—he is of princely extraction.

Ferrandino. Of what country?

Olympia. I know nothing thereof for a

Ferrandino. Meanwhile?

Olympia. But they are also only conjectures!

Ferrandino. Well?

Olympia. Bare conjectures.

Ferrandino. And these?

Olympia. Perhaps he is related to the Grand-master, perhaps to the porte. If his mother was a relation of the Grand-master, then he perhaps is the son of a Sultan; if she was a daughter of a Sultan, then his father perhaps bore the Maltese cross.— But all that is, as before said, merely conjecture. Certainties we have not.

Ferrandino. But his superhuman dissembled age.

Olympia. I know not what to think of it.

Ferrandino. Will the veil of his secrets ever fall?

Olympia. Perhaps.

Ferrandino. Have you grounds to believe so?

Olympia. None.

Ferrandino looked thoughtfully on the ground. Olympia arranged the folds of her garments.

Ferrandino. What do you here?

Olympia. We live, and live happily.

Ferrandino. Without any particular view?

Olympia. Good-living has no other view than that of the good-living itself.

Ferrandino. Has the Old Man any political affairs in Ragusa?

Olympia. I should almost conjecture so.—He often receives visits from the Senators of the city, and they conduct themselves towards him with great submission. He has agents at Algiers, Tunis, Tripoli, Fetz, Malta, and Constantinople. From Egypt and Syria he often receives letters, and even delegates. He also sends some there.—My brother himself was sent by him, a few weeks ago, to Alexandria.—He holds four ships, which under Ragusian colours, navigate almost every sea, and that he trades to China and the Indies I am certain.

She was about to continue, when they saw the Old Man coming towards the pavilion.—They went to meet him. He saluted them compassionately, went with them into the pavilion, and sat himself down by them.

Nikanor. It is a fine morning! Whatever man enjoys of the beauties of a day he enjoys in the morning and the evening, at the coming and parting of day.—And so it is with man. His morning and his evening makes us acquainted with him and his worth. At both coming and parting he is a stranger to dissimulation.—It is only in the middle of his life that time cast a deceitful veil over him. May ours be serene!—are you satisfied with your residence among us?

Ferrandino. Among friends 1 am always satisfied.

Nickanor. Have you, since we last saw each other, form.ed any plans?

Ferrandino. What plan can an exile form? only to endeavour to creep through the world unnoticed.

Nikanor. Then you wish to be again noticed?

Ferrandino. In my former shape? truly not.

Nikanor. But yet in a new one?

Ferrandino. I really do not know what answer to return you. And in what shape could I make myself remarkable? I am unacquainted with any science.

Nikanor. You have judgement, experience and courage,—you could certainly make yourself famed through arms.

Ferrandino. Who would serve under a robber?

Nikanor. You are that no more.—With your revival at Pantilaria you were born anew to the world. You tread a new

sphere like a new man, and your former
faults are expiated by the stab of a poig-
nard. In short you commence a new life.

Ferrandino. Employment I must have.

Nikanor. You shall have some.

A boy entered, and brought Nikanor a
letter   He read it, turned to Olympia, and
said,—

"Your brother begs to be remembered to
you! He is just going as he writes to Ro-
sette, and from thence to Cyrus. From
there we shall again hear from him."

Olympia left the pavilion, as though she
hurried towards some business, and Ferrandino remained with Nikanor.

Ferrandino. Friend! for I—I know not
what to call you.

Nickanor. Call me as you have just
called me, and you will, to your and to my
honor, always call me the best name. But
otherwise you can call me Nikanor.—Yet
what would you say to me?

Ferrandino. I ask you: What shall become of me?

Nickanor. You want employment, you
desire it.—Will you travel?

Ferrandino. Where to?

Nikanor. Have you any inclination for
a sea-faring life?

Ferrandino. No.

Nikanor. To undertake a sort of embassy?

Ferrandino. Where to? and in what concerns?

Nikanor. That will shew itself, in a few days we will speak further of it

As he said this he rose, emptied a glass of milk, and went up to a boy who was coming towards the pavilion. The boy gave him a letter. He went down the grove and was soon out of sight. Ferrandino left the pavilion and went to the orange-arbour and the well-known water-fall.

Serafina sat reading in the arbour.—He went in and spoke to her. She shut the book and, smiling, said,—

"It is a fine morning!"

Laughing, he returned :—

'And it will be a fine day."

Serafina. How have you slept?

Ferrandino. Well, but little.

Serafina. It was just the same with me.

Ferrandino. Certainly, a night-watch of skeletons can enjoy but little agreeable.

Serafina. About the skeletons I troubled myself but little : the lamp plagued me, and I was rejoiced when it was day.

Ferrandino. But what does the night-watching of the skeletons mean?

Serafina. I do not know.

He was about to continue when he perceived Serena.—She saw him and came towards the arbour.—He met her. Laughing she took him by the arm and led him down the grove.

"Already with Serafina again," said she; "that should not be!"

Luigino now met them, and they all three went together to the palace of the Old Man.

Luigino informed Ferrandino he should that evening go to Ragusa, and as soon as possible put to sea again.—Ferrandino requested him, at Palermo, to seek for Fortunata. That he promised, and took his leave of them.

When he had left them, Ferrandino went up to the chamber of the skeletons and found it locked. He asked for Olympia, and was told that she was gone out with the Old Man.

A young man who called himself Fabio asked him if he would accompany him to the chase. He accepted of this invitation, received a gun, and went with him.

He entered a beatiful forest and met company. They divided themselves, and each desirous of a good booty, coursed about according to his judgment.

Ferrandino left the forest to enjoy the prospect of a charming spot.—In the middle stood, on a small eminence, a temple, as it appeared, built in an extraordinary style. He approached it, and near it at a well, saw a girl in a light Grecian habit with a pitcher.

Ferrandino. You draw water here.

Girl. As you see, sir.

Ferrandino. Is the water good?

Girl. Very good. Will you please to taste it?

He drank, and praised the purity of the water.—She took the full pitcher and went towards the temple.

Ferrandino. Do you live here?

Girl. In the yard of the temple with my sisters.

Ferrandino. To whom is the temple dedicated?

Girl. To the King of Heaven, the all enlivening Sun

Ferrandino. Do priests too live here?

Girl. Two old men, dedicated, like us, to the service of the Sun.

Ferrandino. Who built this temple?

Girl. The glorious friend of the godhead, Nikanor the wise.

Ferrandino. Nikanor? and he devoted both you and your sisters to the service of the Sun?

Girl. Himself

Ferrandino. Were you born here :

Girl. I do not know where I was born. At Fronteia I was brought up. I know neither my parents nor my birth-place.

Ferrandino. May any one take a view of the temple?

Girl. None uninitiated dare enter.

Ferrandino. Do you not sometimes come to Nikanor's dwelling?

Girl. Seldom.

He would have questioned her further, but the Old Man coming out of the temple he went towards him.

The Old Man, before he could speak a word called out to him, smiling,—

" The daughters of the sun are beautiful, but not true ?"

Ferrandino would not understand his illusion, but expressed a wish to see the inside of the temple.

" You shall see it," said the Old Man, " though not to-day."

With that he took him by the hand, and led him to a hill planted with myrtles, in whose shades stood a small chapel.

" The myrtles," said he, " are sacred to love, and this chapel is also dedicated to it."

" Are you not a Christian ?"

"I believe myself to be a very good Christian?"

"And sacrifice to heathen deities?"

'Have you never offered to love?"

'Never."

'In no temple."

"Your temples are every where, where you are yourself."

On this he called his attention to the beauty of the surrounding scenery, and led him down into the valley. Here he laid himself under a cypress, and before him six lovely girls danced a Grecian *cotillion*, to the sound of several instruments. After this, his carriage, drawn by four milk-white stags, drove up. He arose and asked Ferrandino if he would ride back with him to the villa.

Ferrandino inquired after Olympia, and was informed that she remained the whole of that day in the temple. Having seated himself by the side of the Old Man, in the carriage, they went towards the villa.

They arrived at dinner-time at the villa. The table was well and heavily laden. Singing, dancing, and music heightened the magnificence of the repast, and the entertainment was lovely and unrestrained. The Old Man proposed riddles, a number of which Serafina knew how to explain.

with great sagacity, whom the Old Man honoured with a bouquet and drank her health.—Singing and music concluded the entertainment, and the company dispersed themselves.

Ferrandino took his guitar, went with it into the garden, hastened to the orange-arbour, and the waterfall, played there, and, by the rustling of the water was soon lulled into a sweet slumber.

When he awoke Serena sat near him, driving away the flies with a sprig of myrtle, and playing with his hair.

She smiled upon him, and he kissed her fragrant lips.

"Why, truly, I shall at last become a complete effeminate here!" said Ferrandino.

Serena lisped to him :

"Remain my lover, and become besides what you will!"

She placed his head on her bosom, held him close, and covered him with kisses.—People came.—She left the arbour and hastened to Serafina's chamber.

Ferrandin again left the arbour of joy, and went to the gallery to see if the chamber of skeletons was open. It was so. The door sprang open. He entered to read the names upon the heads.

The first name which he saw upon a skeleton's head was

ROSALIA.

He started back and sighed deeply—
" Alas, Rosalia !".

He advanced again, read the name a second time, and quickly left the dreadful chamber. In fearful agitation he closed the door behind him and hastened through the gallery to his own chamber

BOOK IV

FERRANDINO again left his chamber and hastened to the Old Man. He found him walking in the garden, surrounded by a great number of male and female scholars, whom he was entertaining with the wonders of nature. He was clad in a blue garment spangled with stars, encircled by a yellow girdle, and a gold chain hung about his neck, to which a saphire enchased with diamonds was suspended. He found him adorned like Doruinrg, teaching in the midst of his pupils of both sexes who were clothed in white; among these were Serena and Serafina.

The Old Man saluted Ferrandino, and continued his discourse.

"Great and wonderful are the works of nature; mighty and adorable is he who has created and preserved them. No mortal can behold him, no mortal can conceal himself from his all seeing eye.—

"Go, ye children of toil! Reflect, examine and weigh well in your heart, all that I have said to you."

They went,—and the Old Man remained alone with Ferrandino.

Nikanor. It seems that, you have been waiting to say something to me?

Ferrandino. I have?

Nikanor. What have you to say to me?

Ferrandino. I was in the Chamber of Skeletons—

Nikanor. Well?

Ferrandino. And on the skull of one of these skeletons the name of Rosalia appeared in terrible characters,—What does that mean?

Nikanor. What should it? It was the custom of the Egyptians to have the skeletons of beloved persons on their tables at a Banquet.—It was the third degree of the Krata Repos, *the Gate of Death*: The initiated, called Melanephoris, were introduced into this chamber, which was filled with embalmed bodies. All the walls were hung full of similar representations.

Ferrandino. And the six skeletons in the dark chamber—?

Nikanor. Are the terrestrial remains of our friends—Men worthy of us.

Ferrandino was silent. The Old Man likewise passed him without uttering a word and walked to a grassy bank where he seated himself whilst Ferrandino leaned against a tree.

Nikanor. The remains of our friends have discomposed you.

Ferrandino. I cannot deny it.

Nikanor. We have young physicians amongst us; whether they study the bones of our friends or strangers is the same.

Ferrandino. Give the remains of your friends to the earth.

Nikanor. Are you a friend to putrefaction?—I am not.—The Celestial is too manifestly disunited from the earthly. What connection can souls have with bones?

Ferrandino. I will not dispute!

Nikanor. What have you?

Both remained silent. The Old Man arose, and went further. Ferrandino walked by his side, with downcast eyes.

Nikanor. 'Tis not well Ferrandino, that you suffer yourself to be so easily dejected; it is not well that you should yet remain so obstinate as you before were. You will now no longer live in obscure caverns and forests, but will mix among mankind, and nothing agrees less with human society than this spirit of obstinacy; mankind do not willingly tolerate it. They either retaliate it, by which you gain nothing—or avoid you and by that you gain still less.

Ferrandino. I feel that you are right.

Nikanor. If you feel that, I have already prevailed on you considerably, and you will follow me—Listen to me and believe me, for I speak from experience.

Ferrandino. Instruct me!

Nikanor. I will intrust you with a secret, and by it discover to you, that of all prudent men, who have been or ever will be of any note in the world. It is called the philosophy of life. Listen to its principles and act according to them.

Ferrandino. You excite my curiosity!

Nikanor. The duties of human society are but an unceasing continuation of exchange. Always employ your understanding, your judgment, your talents, and your complaisance to reciprocal advantage; Do no injury to your neighbours, respect them if they deserve it; serve them, allow them their pretensions and excuse their weaknesses. They are not ungrateful: You will be repaid with two fold interest.

Ferrandino. But there are also friends among these men.—

Nikanor. Certainly!

Ferrandino. And those——?

Nikanor. Ever consider friendship is the most delightful, and at the same time most dangerous gift of Heaven.

Ferrandino. How?

Nikanor. Its charms are transporting, its inconstancy terrible. And can you desire that a wise man will expose himself to the danger of a loss, whose bitterness may poison the remainder of his life?

Ferrandino. What do you say? you contradict yourself, you speak against your own actions.

Nikanor. That only appears so to you.—— Observe this: If your friend meets with a misfortune, which you cannot remedy, spare yourself the pain of seeing him suffer.

Ferrandino. That I cannot!

Nikanor. Every man can do it that will.

Ferrandino. I will not!

Nikanor. That is another thing!

Ferrandino. I must suffer with my friend even though I cannot relieve him, and if he dies and I cannot die with him he leaves me comfortless behind.

Nikanor. It is for children only to weep, and throw away all their play-things because one is taken away from them. What you lose or gain in the world, depends on the favours of fortune. Consider fickle fortune as a ball, on which there is no spot you can safely tread. If fortune steps near you, stretch forth your hand to her; but if she spreads her wings to fly from you, return her gifts and let her fly. You undoubtedly know, what women are, and I hope you understand them!—Fortune too is a woman. Be delighted with her caprice, but never suffer them to deject you.— There are some men who esteem themselves happy because they conceive themselves wise. *Esteem yourself wise when you feel yourself happy.*

He turned himself round and was going but Ferrandino detained him.

Nikanor. What would you? Have I not said enough?

Ferrandino. Enough; enough! And yet not all, that I wish to hear.

Nikanor. And that is?—

Ferrandino. An answer to the question— What is to become of me?

Nikanor. Is not that comprehended in my instructions?

Ferrandino. I not only wish to be instructed, but also to be employed.

Nikanor. I thought you were employed here with Serafina and Serena.

Ferrandino. I leave you.

Nikanor. The girls will weep.

Ferrandino. And you?

Nikanor. I?—I will wish you a prosperous journey.—Whither do you intend to go?

Ferrandino. To unknown countries

Nikanor. Hum!—Have you any inclination to travel to the land of wonders?—to Egypt?

Ferrandino. To Egypt?

Nikanor. A most remarkable country!

Ferrandino. Have you seen it?

Nikanor. I have.

Ferrandino. You have been in Egypt?

Nikanor. As I tell you.

Ferrandino. extraordinary!

Nikanor. That's nothing extraordinary. Many other men have been to Egypt. But who since the Expedition of Alexander can tell us any thing respecting the celebrated temple of Jupiter Ammon? You must visit this.

Ferrandino. Have you seen it?

Nikanor. I have.

Ferrandino. How?

Nikanor. I was initiated there.

In the midst of the boundless sandy deserts of Egypt, are small fertile and inhabited spots called Omiasi, which appear like islands in an unbroken sea. Ammon's Temple stands on one of these islands.—

When Alexander the Great, who was a King in the word's strictest sense, had succeeded iu conquering Egypt, his greatest wish was to visit this temple. With a small part of his army he commenced a journey of sixteen hundred stadia over solitary wilds and burning sands. Surrounded as with a sea they gazed as far as their sight could extend to discover if possible some place that was inhabited. But for some time they could not perceive a single tree, nay, not so much as a blade of grass. At length however, after struggling with innumerable dangers, they arrived at the Oracle which although situated in an almost boundless solitude is nevertheless surrounded with a thick grove, which is watered by several springs of fresh water, and is so very shady as scarcely to be penetrable by the sun's beams. In the midst of this grove near to the temple is a fountain, which at day-break is luke warm, at noon and in the greatest heat, cold; but in the evening it grows warmer insensibly, and at midnight is boiling hot; after this as day approaches, it decreases in heat, and continues this vicissitude for ever.

A boy now approached and brought the Old Man a letter. He opened and read it, and after giving the boy a significant nod to retire, said:

"Ferrandino! To-morrow you are going to Ragusa.—You will there inhabit a house, wel furnished and provided with all the conveniences of life. Make my servants yours. If you should make any stay at Ragusa, you will receive commissions and employment from me. I am now under the necessity of setting out instantly on a small journey.—Farewell and conduct yourself according to the precepts I gave you at Ragusa."

Saying this, he precipitately left him and when Ferrandino returned to the villa, he was told by Serafina that the Old Man had already departed.—Ferrandino was dejected, nor could Serafina herself dispel the gloom that overcast his brow.

Early the next morning he left the villa, and seated himself in a handsome carriage, in which he, accompanied by Fabio, soon reached the city of Ragusa. Fabio rode back again, and Ferrandino made choice of the handsomest chamber in an elegantly furnished house.

He stretched himself on a sofa, and was soon lost in the contemplation of past and passing events, when the steward entered and asked: "In what manner will you please to have the affairs of your house conducted?"

"In the best," replied Ferrandino, who was not less astonished at the question than at the important mein with which it was delivered. But suddenly endeavouring to collect himself, he said, "And so you are the steward?"

"That is the situation I have the honour, to fill, and I dare assert that the sage Nikanor honours me with his confidence;" replied the steward, very submissively, and continued in the same manner :—"Perhaps you would wish to see together the servants of the house?"

"That is not necessary; but——What servants have you here?"

"A valet, two porters, two grooms, a coachman, and eight—"

"Enough! enough!"

"Besides which——, with permission! there are two Circassion ladies in the house."

"How are they employed?"

"According to this letter from the sage Nikanor, they are to expect their employ-ment from you."

"From me?"

"So it stands in the letter."

He took it, read, and found it really was as he said. He returned him the letter, thoughtfully, saying :—

" They shall choose their employments themselves and according to their own tastes."

The valet entered, and announced the Senator Protega.

Ferrandino sprang up and opened the door to him himself.—The steward and the valet retired.—The senator gave Ferrandino his hand, and said :—

" The moment I was informed of your arrival I hurried hither to welcome the friend of the sage Nikanor.

Compliments were exchanged on both sides. They gave mutual assurances of friendship, and at last Ferrandino detained the Senator to supper.

The steward inquired : " If the Circassians might be permitted to wait at table ?"

Ferrandino assented.

The valet entered with a letter from Nikanor to Ferrandino. He read,—

"DEAR FRIEND !

" I forgot to tell you that you are to live at Ragusa, under the name of the knight Artenego. What I have to tell you besides, you shall shortly hear. I once more remind you not to forget the precepts I gave you at Ragusa.   NIKANOR."

The supper was served, and the Circassians, two most lovely girls, entered. Ferrandino's eyes brightened at the prospect; the girls kissed his hands and entreated his favour.

"I assure you of my kindness and attention," said the enraptured Knight.

The Senator, smilingly, threw out a few remarks on the agreeable appearance of the Circassian graces, and they gave themselves up to the pleasures of the table. The girls filled the glasses which were as often emptied with various healths. At last the Senator took a silver drinking-cup, filled with delicious Falernian wine, and said,

"Long life to the handsomest woman in Ragusa!"

"And that," said Ferrandino, "is—"

"In my opinion the Countess Vendramino;" replied the Senator, "and to convince you of my judgment," added he, "I will introduce you to her at a ball which I intend giving a few days hence."

The wine now began to take its effect on the Senator, who placing himself in a sedan was carried in it to his dwelling, and Ferrandino was conducted to his chamber. The valet asked him,

"If the Circassians should sing him to sleep?"

"As I cannot remember that I was ever sung to sleep, I will, on account of its novelty, make a trial of it. They may come and sing."

The maidens entered with harps and seating themselves opposite his couch, played and sung.

Ferrandino slept, and the singers quietly left his chamber.

He awoke, and the handsomest woman in Ragusa fled from him, for she had lived in his dreams the whole of the past night.— He rung. The valet entered.

"Are you of Ragusa?" said Ferrandino to him.

The valet answered in the affirmative. and he said,—

"Who is the handsomest woman in Ragusa?

The valet, without deliberating, replied:

"Certainly the Countess Vendramino!"

Ferrandino paused and arose from his bed. While dressing, this theme was continued.

Ferrandino. Then the Countess Vendramino is really the handsomest woman in Ragusa?

Valet. That's certain! I almost believe that the women themselves will not dispute it.

Ferrandino. That's saying much.

Valet. Much! and yet but little. The Countess is indeed an angel. Several persons, and of distinction' have lost their senses on account of the beauty of the lovely Vendramino.

Ferrandino. Indeed!

Valet. It certainly is true!

Ferrandino. Is she married?

Valet. She was.

Ferrandino. Then her husband is dead?

Valet. Not exactly! Something like it.

Ferrandino. Something like it! Not exactly!

Valet Yes—he disappeared, and no one knows where he went to.—Some time after it was reported that he died in the Baths at Spalatro. That was about three years and a half ago.—Afterwards, a certain Marquis Nardonizzo, with whom she had before been acquainted, went about with her as publicly as though she had been his betrothed: but it did not come to a marriage.

Ferrandino. Was he faithless to her?

Valet. That I do not know. But he went, and no one knows whither. At last it was said, that the Marquis made a journey to Sicily to visit his relations, and was there killed by the Robber-Captain Rinaldini

Ferrandino. By Rinaldini?

Valet. So it was reported.

Ferrandino. That's not true! I don't believe it!

Valet. Neither of us were present; and who knows whether the Marquis ever arrived at Sicily?

Ferrandino. I do not believe it myself!

Valet. Enough! People whisper very strange things of the Countess.

Ferrandino. Do they?

Valet. Yes! but I shall not repeat a word of what I have heard.

The steward now entered, and requested orders. Ferrandino told him he would commit every thing to his judgment; dressed himself hastily, took his hat and sword, and went, unaccompanied, into the city.

After having heard a mass, he went to the harbour, where he amused himself with observing the motley mixture of people of various conditions, ages, and nations. Corsicans' Sicilians, Maltese, Turks, and Britons, were thronging together. Various languages, voices, music, and singing, resounded in the air, and like a masquerade, every one seemed to be in motion, influenced either by restlessness or the power of curiosity. Ferrandino, lost in surprise at this motley scene, stood motionless.

At length he went to a lemon-booth, where
the round fruit brought many pleasing ideas
to his imagination.—A lovely girl was sel-
ling him lemons, when a man muffled up
in a cloak approached him. He heard himself called and turned round. The unknown threw open the cloak and Ferrandino beheld Ludovico.

Without ceremony they embraced, and
the pleasure they felt in again seeing each
other, was expressed in questions of joy.—
They returned together to Ferandino's
dwelling where an excellent breakfast was
served up, and their conversation began
without witnesses.

Ludovico. To see you again among the
living, and to converse with you over this
noble wine—O! it is excess of joy

Ferrandino. Drink, and tell me all that
has past.

Ludovico. I will.——In the dreadful
storm which wrecked our ship, I was thrown
by a wave on some benches and chests,
which with me were cast upon a barren
rock. Here I with difficulty prolonged my
life for three days. On the third I descried
a passing fishing-smack, which perceiving
my signal, made to the rock and took me
in I went with the fisherman to Palmaria,
a small Lipari Isle, where I lived with the

good people above a month. I then resolved to go to Sicily with a Sicilian corn-bark.

I arrived at Palermo, and there I fared wretchedly. I was forced to earn my bread as a porter by the sweat of my brow, and oftentimes had none to eat. What could I do? hunger inspired me with an extraordinary method I went through the streets, crying out that I was a man who was seeking for employment. The invention succeeded. A lady sitting in a balcony, heard me, laughed, spoke to me, and took me in her service. I received a livery and employment. The company which visited Signora Fortunata consisted chiefly of devotees of pleasure.

Ferrandino. Was her name Fortunata?

Ludovico. Yes, her name was Fortunata, and the name of her companion was Fiammetta.

Ferrandino. Fiammetta? it is they

Ludovico. Who?

Ferrandino. Ladies, that I know.

Ludovico. You know them? Who can be certain that you know them!

Ferrandino. Be assured of it, I know them.

Ludovico. They were pretty greenfinches:

Ferrandino. How so?

Ludovico. They understand the arts of pocking.

Ferrandino. How?

Ludovico. Yes, yes! At that time they had got the tender son of the Viceroy of Messina in their clutches and they fleeced him closely. The papa heard of it, and not understanding jesting, had the ladies put in prison.

Ferrandino. Put in prison?

Ludovico. Yes he imprisoned them, and had his son brought to Messina. On this occasion I received five and twenty *ad posteriora*, and was entered as a soldier.— Eight days after I deserted, and crept to our old haunts. I found a few petty thieves but I could not discover any of Rinaldini's company. I therefore went to the harbour and shipped on board a Galley bound to Malta. There I found a Ragusian packet, the same in which I arrived to-day This is the true history of my adventures. I thank Heaven that I am here, and that I have found you!—By what I can see, you live on an easy footing and are a little better lodged than you used to be.—But how are you employed?

Ferrandino. In the sweet indolent occupation of *doing nothing*!

Ludovico. Shame! But I'll wager it will not continue so long.

Ferrandino. Certainly not.

Ludovico. Delightful!—But you will soon undertake something?

Ferrandino. Assuredly:—Have you no inclination to see Egypt?

Ludovico. Egypt? You will hardly go to the land of crocodiles? No, you are a little too prudent to do that.

Ferrandino. Have you no desire to see the temple of Ammon?

Ludovico. No.—But if it must be so,—if—

Ferrandino. The old sage hinted something of that kind.

Ludovico. Where is he?

Ferrandino. He lives in eastern magnificence at a charming villa three miles from here. You shall both see and speak to him to-day.—I have letters for him, which you shall deliver. He will rejoice to see you again.

Fabio was now announced, and entered.

"The illustrious Nikanor," said he, "knows that an old friend, called Ludovico, is with you. He wishes to speak to him, and has therefore despatched me for him."

Ludovico and Ferrandino stared at one another, without knowing what to say. At length Ludovico broke silence:—

"The old man is always the same."

Ferrandino gave him the letters, and Ludovico set out upon his journey with Fabio.

Ferrandino dined with the Senator Protega and was introduced to the acquaintance of a few Ragusian nobles. They spoke of an approaching rupture between Russia and the Turks, of a league of the emperor of Germany with Russia, and supposed that between the two, Ragusa would be crushed. It was reported that the Ottoman would attempt to make inroads in Ragusa; others thought, that Austria would do the same.

Ferrandino tired of this topic longed for its conclusion, and it was not till the repast was nearly ended that he succeeded in giving the conversation a general turn.

After the repast the company separated, and Protega invited Ferrandino to walk with him in his garden without the city. The invitation was accepted and they set out accordingly.

"I have—" said the senator, after they had for some time walked the garden in silence,—" a very handsome female neighbour, the Countess Vendramino, of whom I yesterday spoke to you."

Ferrandino replied smilingly,

"That might endanger yourself more than your garden."

Shall we surprise her?—said Protega; I hope she is here."

Ferrandino did not oppose it, and the intended visit was paid, but—the Countess was in the city.

Evening approached, and they returned to the city.

Ferrandino entertained himself with the Circassions whom he permitted to sup with him; he requested them to sing, and retired to rest that night with unusal spirits.

The following day proved more busy,

After breakfast he sauntered through the city, and was admiring the beautiful structure of St. John's church, when a vulgar fellow came reeling from a tavern towards him. He stepped on one side, to let him pass, while the man stood still and, staring him full in the face, exclaimed, by God! look at this man, and you see in him the famous Rinaldini in propria persona.

Ferrandino hastily stepped up to him, and said:

."Have you known the man whom you just named?"

"I have known him;" said he, quite dryly.

"It is the wine that makes you lie.'

"Sir! The wine does not lie. Wine utters truth."

"Go home, and sleep yourself sober."

'What? Sir? what do you say? that I am drunk?—damnation! I, will roar like a—I will roar that the whole city may hear it—the Robber-Captain Rinaldini resembles you."

A croud soon gathered round the fellow, and asked: what was the matter?

Ferrandino holding all explanations as superfluous, cooly said,—

"The man is drunk," and, to avoid the mob, entered the next house.

Here a servant came towards him, and inquired if he wished to speak to the Countess?

"Who inhabits this house?"

"The Countess Vendramino."

Ferrandino knew not what to answer: just at this moment the Senator Protega entered the house. He looked at him with a smile, and called to him:

'Look there, Knight!"

Ferrandino endeavoured to speak, but the Senator continued :—

"Permit me to introduce you to the Countess."

"I have indeed," stammered Ferrandino, "to scape only a trifling embarrassment, entangled myself in a greater one."

"How so?"

"To avoid some drunken sailors, who were staggering along the street, I came into this house; learn that it is the residence of the Countess Vendramino; see you enter, and am to be introduced to a lady, whom I——."

"That's pleasant," cried a young man who was just then entering the house, "without are a great body of people standing in a circle round a man who swears that the celebrated Rinaldini is gone into this house."

"What?" said Protega, "Rinaldini in this house? Is the man foolish?"

The servant, who was looking out cried,——

"The guard is coming."

"What's the guard to us," replied the Senator. "Only follow me, Knight, without ceremony!" saying this, he took him by the hand and conducted him up stairs.

"By God! Senator!" said the young man, "the guards are there."

Without saying a word, Protega opened a door, and went with Ferrandino across a hall to a chamber, threw open the door, and said to a girl, who was coming towards him,——

"Conduct this gentleman immediately to the Countess!" and again returned

The girl looked irresolutely at Ferrandino; and he, in an agitated tone, said,—

"Dear child! do not yet conduct me to the Countess, I am——I must first collect myself."

"Something unpleasant it seems has happened to you!" said the girl, affectionately.

"It is nothing," stammered Ferrandino,

The door then opened. A lady stood at the door. The girl called to him:—

"The Countess?"

Ferrandino bowed as confused and awkwardly as possible, and the girl continued:—

"The Senator Protega desired me to present this gentleman to you."

The countess retired a few paces into the chamber, observed the confusion of the stranger, became confused herself, and at length she said,—

'Will you not come nearer?"

Ferrandino instantly went into the chamber, and seizing the hand of the Countess, said,—

"The Senator Protega must and will excuse all, that now passes contrary to etiquette and custom. An extraordinary event embarrasses me, and brings me hither. I am the Knight Artenego?"

"O, then!" said the Countess, pleasantly, "the Knight Artenego is welcome."

"No, farther," cried a voice at some distance; "it is an insult to the Countess."

What is that?" said the Countess, anxiously, and pulled the bell.

The door opened; an officer entered the hall; the servants of the Countess thronged after him.

"Sir," said the Countess, "what do you look for here?"

"I beg your pardon!" said the Officer. "I ask for nothing more. I have found what I sought after."

"And that," said the Countess, "is——!"

The Officer turned to Ferrandino, and said,—

"Sir, your sword! you are my prisoner!"

"I?" said Ferrandino, with firmness.

Officer. You.

Countess. The Knight Artenego?

Officer. This gentleman.

Countess. He is a relation of mine.

Officer. Countess!

Ferrandino. Where is the Senator Protega?

Officer. I know not.

Ferrandino. He knows me; he knows who I am.

Officer. You may be who and what you

will. I have orders to arrest you. Now ask no more, but follow me.

Countess. Publicly! through the streets?

Officer. Will you lend us your carriage?

Countess. I will; but first permit me to call the Senator Protega hither.

Officer. I have no orders to do that. The gentleman will follow me without further delay, and if he really is your relation, he will prove himself such. But till then, we shall believe him to have deceived you, and to be neither your relation nor really a Knight, but the famous Robber-Captain Rinaldini!

Countess. Gracious Heaven! Knight! You?—Speak! Are you the Knight Artenego?

Ferrandino. I am.

Countess. And would you attach so dishonourable a name to a man of condition?

Officer. I only act according to my orders. This gentleman, whoever he is, must follow me!

Countess. Sir! but do you know that you dare not violate the rights of my house? My house is a free house!

Officer. As long only as the Senate finds it convenient to esteem it such.

Countess. That would be an extraordinary privilege! but the Senate must first explain this to me themselves. Till then I will suffer no encroachment on my rights.

Officer. My order purports, that I am to arrest this man in this house, and he must follow me immediately.—Guards

The guards entered.

Countess. Lieutenant! not a step further! You shall not, and dare not infringe on the rights of my house. They are rights which my forefathers have received for important services rendered to the Senate. The order that suffers you to make encroachment on these rights, must be drawn up in writing and signed by the Senate. Now will I immediately repair to the ruler of the Republic, and represent the circumstance to him myself. Till then, and till I have received an answer, the Knight remains unmolested in my house, even though he really was the person you take him for, but who has long ceased to be among the living.

Officer. I received my orders from my commander. He is responsible for what he has commanded. I know my duty and obey.—Sir! follow me, and do not constrain us to use violence.

Countess. No! he shall not follow you.

Officer. Countess!

Countess. I will not permit the rights of my house, privileges granted by the city, to be invaded. And, if you will use force, you must first lay hands on me. Here stand my servants; venture not to abuse me. By Heaven, let what will happen, though blood should be spilt, you are answerable for all ! but a republican will not be deprived of her rights, if she is not at the same time robbed of her liberty or her life. A free city must remain sacred.

Officer. Though I found him at an altar, I would perform what I was commanded. For the last time, follow me.

Countess. No !.

Ferrandino. I do not oppose your orders, but I will defend the rights of the countess with my sword to the last drop of my blood.

Officer. Will you dare do that?

Ferrandino. I dare.

" What will you do?" said a loud voice.

All eyes were turned towards the inquirer, and the Old Man of Fronteia, dressed in all the splendour of the East, entered the room, followed by sixteen Moors.

" Prince," cried the countess, flying to him, "you must know—"

" I know all," replied the Old Man, and pressed her hand.

All were astonished, and the officer stood before him speechless.

The Old Man still kept the same serene and unchanged countenance and continued:

"Artenego! My son, Ferrandino! yield to the power of your superiors—Surrender your sword, suffer yourself to be quietly brought before the Senate, to what is there said to you, reply with modesty and calmness, and expect the triumph of your acquittal. You, Countess, will announce to the Senate what has happened.

"But this officer must obey his order. You, my son, will follow him, the chariot is at the door; and you can make use of it."

Ferrandino.   But do you know—

Nikanor.   What should I not know?

Countess.   It is supposed—

Nikanor.   That this honourable man is Rinaldini—I know it.

Countess.   And—

Nikanor.   He is not.

Countess.   Certainly not?

Nikanor.   Chance often produces stranger events from similarity of features. Many a man has been brought into difficulties from his appearance—But that is nothing to the purpose. I know the knight—

Countess. But, Prince! You must know,

Nikanor Oh! I know many things— But innocence must speak for itself In the mean time something must be done immediately for this young man. I have been in his house and understanding what had happened brought his papers in proof of his rank. They are sealed. Lieutenant! you will deliver them at the same time with your prisoner.—Now go!—or we shall not be able to dine together this afternoor

Countess. We?

Nikanor. We!

Countess. With the Knight?

Nikanor. With the Knight; and indeed here with you—Go, my son!

Ferrandino in confusion and busied more with the Old Man and his proceedings than with his own adventures, resigned his sword, and followed him and the guards—They were just leaving the hall, when two Senators entered. They delivered an order from the Senate to the Countess. She read it, and very composedly said:

" I submit to the commands of the Senate, and the Knight already follows the guard !"

" Now,"—said the Old Man to the officer, " deliver these papers to the Senators immediately. It will spare the Knight some trouble."

The Officer gave the papers to the Senate.

They broke the seal, read a few words, returned the papers to the Old Man, and said to the Officer:

"The Knight will not follow you, you have done your duty.—For the rest we are answerable."

The Officer returned his sword to Ferrandino and led off the guard.

The Old Man retired with the Senators to a chamber.

The eyes of the Countess were fixed on Ferrandino, while his were cast on the ground; all the others remained immoveable, and the deepest silence succeeded this scene of tumult.

The Countess at length dismissed her servants, who, with the Old Man's Moors, left the hall. The approached Ferrandino and said: Do we—?

He slowly raised his eyes, and said:

"How often do realities resemble illusive dreams! They but make amends for melancholy realities that dispel them."

Countess. What, nothing more?

Ferrandino. Than what?

Countess. A sigh is too little for all that has passed.

Ferrandino. I will pay two-fold, when I have regained my breath

Countess. Me or the Prince?

Ferrandino. Both.

She smiled, and left the hall. Ferrandino remained, lost in thought, behind. "Prince," said he to himself, ' the Countess calls the Old Man Prince—He entered in the pomp and splendour of a Sultan; with but a single word from him the Senators gave freedom to a man to secure whose person they even made search in a free city. How? have I not always taken this man for a Charlatan? and have I erred? Should Olympia's inconsiderate conjectures be perhaps realities—Should they be truths? But whence—wherefore. does he do all this, for me? for me?"

The door of the chamber in which the Old Man and the Senators had entered, opened and they came forward.

The Old Man went towards Ferrandino, and kindly said to him:

"My son! prepare yourself for travelling:" and went across the hall to the chamber into which the Countess had before entered. The Senators followed him.

"Prepare for travelling!" said Ferrandino, and remained behind, surprised and motionless.

Meanwhile the Senator Protega entered the hall

"Knight!" said he, "you are rescued. It is fortunate that the Prince happened to come to town just then! Where is he?"

Ferrandino silently pointed to the chamber he had just entered, and Protega was going into it, when the Old Man left it.

"It is all settled," said the Old Man, smiling. "Nothing shall now spoil our dinner."

"Your commissions," said Protega, "Are executed."

"Good."

"Every thing is ready."

"I thank you——Yet go for a moment to the Countess."

Protega went, and the Old Man, requested Ferrandino to follow him into a chamber—He did so.

Nikanor. You were in a dangerous situation, my son!

Ferrandino. And how could you save me?

Nikanor. By a few words, as you witnessed.

Ferrandino. My thanks——

Nikanor. Let them rest!

Ferrandino. Permit me to ask a question.

Nikanor. Well?

Ferrandino. You are here universally called Prince. Are you——

Nikanor. A Prince?

Ferrandino. That is my question

Nikanor. I am.

Ferrandino. But——

Nikanor. We shall dine together—— After our repast Protega will conduct you to the harbour. There you will go on board a packet which is to convey you to Dalmatia. You will then be conducted to a castle of the Countess Vendramino's. For some time you can live there, till you receive from me the plan of your future conduct.

Ferrandino. You promised me employment.

Nikanor. By this time you would have received it, had not your countenance so unseasonably brought you into trouble. At present we must think of something else.

He took him by the hand, and led him to the dining-room, into which the Countess soon after came with the Senator.

They seated themselves at table. The Old man was very cheerful, and talked much. Protega was the same, the Countess spoke little, and Ferrandino scarcely at all.

Children!—said the Old Man,—you are melancholy. But you will not always be so.   I hope soon to see you very talkative

After dinner Ferrandino took his leave.
The Old Man wished him a happy voyage,
the Countess did the same, and affectionately squeezing his hand, said,

"We shall soon see one another again!"

Ferrandino went with Protega to the harbour entered on board a vessel in which he
found his things well packed and in the
best order—Protega bade him adieu and
returned, while the vessel put to sea.

BOOK V

Ferrandino was landed between Cipichio vechio and Casa tosana Two servants of the Countess accompanied him and carried his luggage after him. At Tolone, they bought mules, and leaving the mountains of Comcerusi and Lazano on the left, reached the fortified Castle Ostrosine, which lay on the left of a mountain, and belonged to the Countess. The servants delivered a letter to the steward of the castle, requested an attestation from Ferrandino, that they had brought him safely to the destined place, received it, and well rewarded by him for their voyage, returned back in the vessel.

Toroneto, the steward of the castle, received his guest very politely.

"Sir Knight!"—said he—" you are welcome to Ostrosine. The Countess writes to me that I am to regard you as the lord of this castle, and I shall omit nothing that may convince you of my most punctual attentions.

Margalisa, the steward's sister, a rustic lively creature, shewed the guest his chamber, which was very conveniently and tastily furnished.

"Is the Countess often here?" said he.

'Generally six weeks in the year, in summer,—replied Margalisa."

Ferrandino. You have here the prospect of an enchantging country.

Margalisa. O! undoubtedly, the country is fine, the prospect is charming, but like every thing else, which one sees daily, one gets accustomed to it, one's looking-glass not excepted.

Ferrandino. You look diligently then in your look-ing-glass?

Margalisa. Usually every day, but only in the morning, unless I chance to make myself dirty in the kitchen. But on a Sunday when I go to church, it happens a few times more.

Ferrandino. Is the church far from here?

Margalisa. I walk it in an hour. But I am a good walker. My brother takes longer—There lies our Parsonage, in the midst of yon thicket.

Ferrandino. You are very religious then in this neighbourhood.

Margalisa. O yes! at least more so than the citizens.—A pleasant gentleman once lived here for twelve weeks and during the whole time he did not so much as once visit our church.

Ferrandino. Who was this pleasant gentleman?

Margalisa The Countess sent him here with a letter also, in the same manner as she has you. He was called the Marquis Nardonizzo.

Ferrandino. Nardonizzo?

Margalisa. Did you know him

Ferrandino. No.

He thought in silence on what the valet at Ragusa had related to him of the Marquis Nardonizza, and Margalisa came nearer to him at the window.

Margalisa. Do you intend to stay long with us at the castle?

Ferrandino. I do not yet know myself.

Margalisa. Will the Countess meanwhile also come here?

Ferrandino. I believe she will.

Margalisa. Indeed? Then will every thing be again lively. As long as she is not here, I, my brother, his wife, two children and a maid-servant, live like hermits. One day passes like another. The little work is soon done, and then one's time wears very heavy. It is detestable to be stuck in such a solitary castle on a mountain.

Ferrandino. That I believe.

Margalisa. So you will find it, if you remain here long. You will certainly have many weary hours.

Ferrandino You will be here.

Margalisa. What can that help you? I cannot divert you.

Ferrandino. Faith very well?

Margalisa. With what?

Ferrandino. You will relate to me——

Margalisa. What?

Ferrandino. Tales of all kinds—of this castle.

Margalisa. Of our castle? I know very little of it myself. My brother knows more.

Ferrandino. What then?

Margalisa. O? this and that—our castle has also its secrets. But I am not acquainted with them.

Ferrandino. Secrets?

Margalisa. I do not willingly speak of them

Ferrandino. Why not?

Margalisa. Because I do not know any of them for certain.

Ferrandino. I too have heard many of them.

Margalisa. What then?

Ferrandino. It is reported that all is not as it should be.

Margalisa looked about her cautiously, went up to him, laid her hand upon his shoulder, looked at him kindly, and said: "say nothing of it!"

Ferrandino looked at her affectionately, and in the same manner said,

"I know,—what I know?"

She took her hand from his shoulder, seized the lappel of his coat, cast down her eyes, and lisped—

'I have said nothing—and," added she quickly, "I also know nothing. You perhaps know more than I do."

Ferrandino tapped her cheek, raised up her face and smiling replied:

I believe that myself!"

"I do not know what you may think of me,"—said she, "but it is certain, that I am good, and mean better than many ladies of distinction."

With that she sprang out of the room.

Ferrandino considered Margalisa's hints compared them with the relations of the valet at Ragusa, and combined out of them many prejudicial conjectures.—The Steward appeared to be a very reserved man, and towards him he conducted himself with equal reserve, but he hoped to learn all by degrees from Margalisa; he therefore behaved very politely to her, which he did not find at all difficult to do, as she was in reality a handsome girl, and in the loneliness of a castle her charms were doubly alluring, he presented her with a necklace and a ring. These presents were received as willingly as they were given, and Ferrandino already perceived by the attention with which he was served, that the golden chain had fettered the love of Margalisa.

After he had remained there a few days, he despatched a letter to the Old Man, in which he earnestly entreated him to give him employment. He also requested him to send Ludovico to him.

His intimacy with Margalisa increased daily, and his friendly manners at last made her look upon him in a very different light, his presents and the loneliness of the place had also their effects, and the Knight began to spend his time very agreeably.

It pleased the girl and pleased the Knight. Thus they were contented with each other.

Once, as she was sitting by him in a pensive mood, she asked him smiling, and with naivette,

"How many do I make, that have loved you?"

The Knight, in truth a little more subtle than the open-hearted girl, knew how to evade this question by a method which we would reccommend as very useful to him, who may be at a loss how to answer a question from a pretty woman.—He therefore asked,

"How many besides myself have loved you?"

This made her forget her own question, she blushed more deeply than before, cast down her eyes, and played with her hand-kerchief.

Emboldened by her confusion, Ferrandino forgot every answer, and confidently repeated his question, while he turned Margalisa's countenance towards him.

She was almost offended with him, but she stifled her vexation, and replied in tears.

"You are the third of my lovers, but the only one who has received from me more than kisses."

She paused, but quickly continued, and almost angry asked him:

"Do you believe it,"

"I not only believe it,"—said Ferrandino quite composedly, "but I am also con- vinced of it."

'Heaven inspired you to say that!" said she suddenly, at the same time hiding in her bosom beneath a handkerchief, some- thing that she had kept in her right hand.

"What is that?"—said Ferrandino—and wrestling with her, he drew a dagger out of her bosom.

Ferrandino. It was this you grasped in your hand, and thrust into your bosom.

Margalisa. It was.

Ferrandino. Margalisa!

Margalisa. I have given to you, what I cannot again give to any man. Had you been so indiscreet as to deny this gift, I should have closed your lips for ever, that you ingrate, might never be capable of again denying any thing—I have acted imprudently, but—I will not suffer myself to be insulted.

Ferrandino perceived that he had to do with a girl whose resolution equalled his assurance. He soon determined how to act; he threw his arms round her neck kissed her vehemently, and said,

"Margalisa! I now love you!"

She was silent, and big tears fell from her eyes. At length she said almost piti- fully, "I know that I am unhappy, but I

also know that you will be unhappy with me, if you forget, that it is you who have made me so."

Ferrandino had never heard any girl speak so before. All his mistresses had wept after him, but none had ever followed him with daggers. He however quickly collected himself, kissed her more tenderly, and said :

" Be composed, Margalisa ! I shall never forget what I am indebted to you."

Just at this moment they heard a noise in the hall, near the chamber in which they were.

" What is that ?"—said Ferrandino.

Margalisa started up, and cried,

" Ah ! that is the unlucky hall !" and rushed out of the chamber.

Ferrandino, lost in surprise, remained behind. He listened but he could hear nothing more. He placed his ear to the hall door; nothing was moving there.

He now left the castle, and wandered round the neighbourhood for about an hour; here he enjoyed the splendid prospect of the setting sun, a prospect which always left behind melancholy sensations in his soul, and went slowly back to the castle— At the draw-bridge he once more looked back to the valley, which was already darkened by the shadow of evening, he sighed,

"There was a time when in the close of evening I drove back my goats to our little cot, and then I was cheerful and happy. I now look from proud castles down upon the valley, and the veil of twilight wraps my soul in melancholy."

He staggered back to his lonely chamber in the castle, found the table covered, and Margalisa soon after brought in supper. He emptied a glass of wine, and called for a second—Margalisa brought it him.

"You must drink with me," said he, "You must remain with me. It is too lonely for me; I am out of spirits."

Margalisa. That is not well. Can I raise your spirits?

Ferrandino. You alone can do it.

Margalisa. When I have finished my work, I will come again. But you must sing something to me. You sing so very prettily and know such pleasant songs. I have already learnt some of them from you. "The Fishing Girl," and the "Melancholy Knight of the Rocky Vale."

Ferrandino. Only come again. I will sing you songs and romances.

Margalisa. In an hour I will be here again.

She went——When the hour had elapsed she returned again——She seated herself with her knitting needles on a sofa, and Ferrandino walked up and down the room humming on a guitar.

"Has the Countess," said Margalisa carelessly, written to you ?"

" No."

" My brother supposed she would probably soon come here."

" So ?"

A pause.

" But you expect her?"—said Margalisa.

" No."

" Not ?—really not? and you are here ?'

" The expectation of her arrival is not the motive."

A second and yet longer pause.

Ferrandino interrupted it.

" Do any villages belong to the castle of the Countess "

" Two—the village in the thicket, and that to the right of the great pond."

" Are there any convents in the neighbourhood ?"

" About an hour's walk from here is a convent of Nuns, of the holy Clara ; two hours distant is a Capuchin convent. I know no other convent besides in the neighbourhood. In the convent of St Clara I have a sister. She is Portress.'

"You visit her sometimes?"

"Usually three times a year, at the high feast. It may be my fate to enter a convent. Commonly nothing more than a convent is left to a poor girl, if she cannot get a husband."

"That will not be-your ease!"

"Oh! indeed! Men with us are to be had but now and then!"

Here ensued a third pause.

Margalisa at length said,—

"What disturbs you? Sing something You promised me you would."

Ferrandino considered a little, preluded, and then sung :—

"Margalisa is the girl I love."

"Have you made that yourself?" said Margalisa.

"I composed it while singing.'

"Aha! Do you know what it says in a song you often sing? It says——

"Hush," said Ferrandino, laughing, and laid down the guitar. He threw his arms round Margalisa's neck, and said,—

"Then I will speak the truth. I love you."

Margalisa sighed,—

"How long will you love me?"

They heard footsteps. Margalisa started up and set herself on a stool.

Ferrandino took the guitar and hummed.
The Castellan entered the chamber.

"I come to ask you," said he, "if you have any commands for Ragusa? A ship lies at Cosa Rosana, which is going there, and I shall send many things myself."

Ferrandino wrote a letter to the Old Man, in which he renewed the request of the last letter.

Margalisa, who in the meanwhile had left the room with her brother, returned when Ferrandino rang. He gave her the letter, and requested her to come back.

"My brother," replied she, "is going to Cosa Rosana himself to-night. When he is gone, I will come."

She went, and Ferrandino, to whom her company had become indispensable, expected her return with impatience.

Towards evening he went to the window, and looked down towards the valley. The moon illuminated the whole region, and he perceived at the foot of the mountain a heavy loaded wagon, and men walking to and fro. These soon ascended the mountain, and entered the castle. When they again descended, they carried what appeared to be small casks, with no inconsiderable exertion of their own strength. They once more ascended, and returned laden in the same manner as before. The steward went with them, conducting his horse down the mountain, which he mounted in the valley. The casks were laid on the wagon, and the caravan proceeded through the valley on the right. The conductors of the wagon were, like the inhabitants of that part, chiefly Morlacks, the Häiducks, and the Dalmatians, armed according to the custom of their country.

Margalisa soon after entered the chamber.

"Is your brother gone?"

'He is."

"What did they carry down the mountain in those casks?"

"I do not know."

"You are not sincere."

"It is just because I am candid," said she, "that I do not know. My brother tells us nothing of his affairs. Such casks are often carried away from here. I neither know from whence they come, nor what is in them. They are very heavy, You know that I have strength, but I cannot lift any of them."

"Extraordinary!"

"Yes; in our castle there are many extraordinary things, of which I know nothing. My brother is very mysterious, and we women, who have the misfortune to be deemed indiscreet, are not intrusted with any of his secrets."

" Then he has secrets?"

" That I should suppose."

" I am not inquisitive, but still the casks interest me."

" They have already interested me a long while; particularly as I do not see them brought into the castle, and yet they are there, and are sent away."

Ferrandino threw himself on the couch. Margalisa seated herself by him, and played with her hair.

Margalisa. You are still thinking of the casks. I too have often thought of them, very often; but all that has not helped me.

Ferrandino. Do you not know any of the secrets of the hall, which you called the unlucky hall.

Margalisa. My brother always calls it the unlucky hall, but never says why, and keeps it fast locked up. There is something mysterious in it. Who knows what demon haunts it?

Ferrandino. Do you believe in ghosts?

Margalisa. Ha! Who will not believe in them? Alas! in our country there are but too many ghosts and witches.

Ferrandino. Witches too?

Margalisa. Yes! I will relate to you, what a Franciscan monk himself saw, heard, and discovered to a gentleman of distinction.

Ferrandino. Well?

Margalisa. A handsome young gentleman fell into the hands of some witches, who, during his sleep, took his heart out of his body which they roasted, intending to make a delicious repast of it. He did not perceive his loss, because he, as I before said, was asleep. But when he awoke, he began to feel a pain, and at last discovered he had lost his heart. The Franciscan monk, who lay in the same chamber, beheld all, and knew what the sorceresses had done, but could not prevent them, because they had enchanted him. At length, when the young man awoke, the whole enchantment was undone. The witches anointed themselves with oil, and flew away. But the Franciscan took the heart, which was already roasted, from the gridiron and gave it to the young man to eat: and he then, with God's help, became healthy.

Ferrandino. A terrible adventure!

Margalisa. It was indeed!

Ferrandino. How long will your brother be away?

Margalisa. Two days.

Ferrandino. Could you not procure me the keys to the hall?

Margalisa. What a request you make to me! 1 must not love you at all, were I o procure you the keys you ask.

Ferrandino. If you love me, procure them for me.

Margalisa. No! I will not contribute any thing to your misfortunes.

Ferrandino. Does your brother go into the hall?

Margalisa. I believe so!

Ferrandino. And nothing happens to him? neither will any thing happen to me.

Margalisa. He has a great many medals.

Ferrandion. What are they?

Margalisa. I will shew you, see, here on my frill is a Zapitz.

It was a scrip of paper, written over with holy names and unmeaning characters. The priests sold them to the superstitious Morlacks and Dalmatians as a preservative against ghost and enchantments.

" An on my necklace,"—continued she,—" hangs a Petitz."

This was a coin with the picture of the Virgin Mary and the Infant.

"Oh!—said Ferrandino smiling,—I have

enough of the same kind of Zapitzes and Petitzes!"

"Really?"—said Margalisa, astonished

"Enough!—If they will protect me, you may give me the keys, and nothing unpleasant will befall me."

Margalisa And yet I will not trust them!

Ferrandino. Then your Zapitzes and Pititzes are also worth nothing.

Margalisa. O yes! But—if you should be unfortunate, I should not know what to do.—And even if I wished to give you the keys, I do not know where to find them. My brother has undoubtedly locked them up.

Just then they heard a noise. They listened and distinctly heard that it was in the hall.—Margalisa leaned tremblingly on Ferrandino, and he beckoned to her to be silent.

Ferrandino raised himself softly, ascended, and listened.—All was silent.

He returned. Margalisa fearfully declared, that she would not go out of the chamber that night. Ferrandino laughed, and left the chamber with her. They went through the second into the third chamber, and here Margalisa became more easy, as if she were in greater security at a little

distance from the hall than when near it.—
But before she left him, Ferrandino was
obliged to accompany her down stairs to
her chamber, which was the lowest story
in the castle.

When he returned to his chamber his
eyes fell on his portmanteau, which since
his arrival at the castle he had not opened,
and it immediately occured to him, that he
had very good pick-lock instruments in it,
which Ludovico had given him to take
care of, when he sent him from Ragusa to
the Old man.—He opened the portmanteau,
took out the implements of former dexteri-
ty, and determined immediately to unfold
the secrets of the unlucky hall.

He quickly went to work, armed himself,
and approached the hall door with two
burning wax-lights.

The excellency of his instruments crown-
ed his first effort with success. The locks
were opened and the hall doors fell back.—
In the hall it was still and dark ; the win-
dows opened to gardens, imperceptible to
the smallest rays of the moon.

Ferrandino entered the hall, which was
empty and unfurnished. Two folding doors
presented themselves on the right, which
were simply locked and soon gave way to
the expert pick-lock. They led to a long

gallery, which was ornimented on both sides with pictures, and provided with wall candlesticks.

In these branches were the remains of candles, which to all appearance had been recently lighted.

"Then there are men here,"—said Fer randino to himself, "for ghosts do not require these lights!"

With firm steps and gentle pace he advanced, and came, at the end of the gallery, to a similar door which was locked. He opened it and entered into a small hall, the walls of which were likewise hung with lights and pictures.

An opened door led him to a chamber This was furnished, and shewed signs that it was visited by men.—Ferrandino now advanced cautiously, and from the chamber came to a small dark arched avenue.

Here he stopped and debated with himself whether he should proceed, or suspend his further research till the morrow. He lingeringly advanced by degrees, and was still pondering when he trod on something pliant, on which a bell loudly echoed through the castle vaults, and it slowly sunk with him to a great depth.

When he stood on firm ground, he found himself in an extensive vault, but faintly illumininated by a few suspended lamps, and perceived the sinking machine slowly re-ascend.—

There was now no thinking of return.

He stood, listened and heard at a distance a noise like that of stamping-machines and wheel-works turned by water.

"Should I approach the noisy work of Danaides, the wheel of Ixion, and the horrors of———, or an Orcus of the Krata Repoa—said he to himself—I will go forward."

He took the light in the left hand, and in the right held a cocked pistol, and advanced.—The further he went the more distinctly he heard the noise.

A door arrested his progress. He resolutly opened it and entered a second vault better lighted up, but lower; he had scarcely set his foot in this, when he perceived a figure who at his appearance loudly hallooed "Alarm!" and ran away.

He stopped, secured his back, placed the lights near him on the ground, put himself in an armed position, and awaited the event.

A dark-clothed man with white hair and beard came towards him, and thundered out:

"Rash man! who art thou? how camest thou here? and what dost thou seek here?"

Ferrandino calmly replied :

" I ask you : who art thou ? after your answer mine will follow."

The Old Man paused a few moments and again asked :

" Are you here alone ?"

" That you will learn,"—was Ferrandino's answer.

" You, with all your followers that are buried in these vaults are in my power, and you will never again leave this place, if I do not let you free.—Therefore answer man ! who art thou ?"

" A man, as you have said. Or do you not believē; than there is a man who came here without fear ?"

" You have ventured much !"

" And not enough."

" What more ?"

" That you shall learn."

Ferrandino rushed at him, seized him by the throat, pressed him against the wall, and pointed the pistol to his breast.

The Old Man trembled and remained silent.

But Ferrandino repeated the question :
" Who art thou ?"

The old man returned no answer.—Ferrandino shook him, and cried out to him :

" Answer my question, or I will shoot you."

" That you may do," said the Old Man, " if you will give up your own life for lost. Answer my, question and I will answer yours. I clearly perceive that I have to do with a courageous determined man, but notwithstanding I do not fear you."

" False !" cried Ferrandino—"you trem-ble."

" I am," continued the Old Man—"old and feeble, and you are superior to me in corporeal strength, for thou art young and strong ; men are near. With these you must contend if you would conquer with honor."

Ferrandino released him, and was just going to speak, when he saw three men coming towards him with naked sabres.

" Seize," cried the Old Man, when he perceived them, and found himself free— " this madman !"

To Ferrandino he said,

If you defend yourself, you shall be cut down.

" If you can answer that to the Countess Vendramino, whose brother I am,"—said Ferrandino,—" you may cut me down ; but I shall defend myself as long as I can move a limb, and if any one approaches me, I will shoot *you* the first."

" Stop !"—cried one of the three,—"this

voice is well known to me. And this countenance.—I'll be shot! if you are not Rinaldini."

" Your name?" said Ferrandino.

" Nero."

" Nero! You?"

" It is not true, you are—"

" I am—I am your captain and command you and your comrades to lay down your arms."

" Come, my brave companions!" cried Nero, " hear my captain's command, have respect and lay down your arms. Here stands the great Rinaldini and speaks to you."

" Silence!" thundered out the Old Man.

" What?—do you want?—I will stand by my captain, fight and die with him. But come only once too near us, if you would learn the consequences of fighting with the great Rinaldini!"

" Let them come on, said Ferrandino, " we will receive them warmly. My people in the castle will seek me, and we shall soon receive assistance, '

" Shut the trap-doors," cried the Old Man.

" Useless precaution!" said Ferrandino, " no locks are to fast for my people."

" That we shall see," said the Old Man.

Several men rushed by just then out of the vaults through which Ferrandino had entered, crying.

"Alarm! alarm! The castle is surprised; soldiers have possessed it. We are discovered and lost."

"Save yourselves," cried the Old Man.

Nero took Ferrandino by the hand, and said, "Follow me."

In the subterraneous recesses, the confusion was universal. Ferrandino thought he heard the voices of women and crying of children. He was led upwards, and through a lumber room. Nero whispered to him:

"No one knows this way but myself and Rodosla—We discovered it but three days since, and kept the discovery secret, having long thought that the business would at some time have a bad end."

Nero directly after called to him:

"Now you must creep on all fours."

In this manner they crept through the mouth of a frightful cavern in the rocks, whose outlet led to an extensive rugged, mountainous region.

They were scarcely in the open air, when another man crept out.

"That is Rodosla, my comrade," said Nero,—"a brave and valiant Haiduck."

Rodosla was scarcely out, when he

Nero as previously agreed, rolled without saying a word, a large fragment of rock before the outlet of the cave.—He then remained standing, and stared at Ferandino.

Rodosla. Nero! what is that? who is this man? he is not one of us, does not belong to us.

Nero, You shall soon know him better, Rodosla!

Rodosla. I cannot conceive———how came he to us?

Nero. You shall know all, have but patience.

Ferrandino. Be assured, noble Rodoslal that my presence will bring with it any disadvantage to you.—But what is to be done now?

Nero. That must be well considered of.

Rodosla. First of all I will, as I am acquainted with this region and the impassible tracts, see if we can venture in the valley.

Ferrandino. Very right!

Nero. You will do well!

Without further deliberation, Rodosla crept onward between rocks and bushes which soon hid him from their sight.

" Now tell me, Captain!"—said Nero—"what brought you into our cave."

Ferrandino gave him an account of as much as he wished him to know.

Nero. Zounds ! how glad 1 am to see you again :—that you again recovered and was restored to life, I already knew in Sicily , but it was reported among us, that you had entered a convent. That I would not at first believe, but as I neither heard nor saw any thing of you, I began to think it possible that you had changed the sword for the paternoster, to reconcile yourself and us to heaven.—I abandoned the old trade, but nothing was to be gained by that. At length I unexpectedly fell in with Cinthio, who persuaded me to go with him to Ragusa. There he stuck me in a company of pirates, and we cruised about in search of booty—once when we returned from one of these incursions, I presented myself to the Old Man of Fronteia, whom they call Prince. I found many old acquaintances there ; among others the Signora Olympia, Serena, Astolfo, and also our Luigino. They made me many eulogiums, and at last spoke of a secret expedition. I wondered what it would produce, and promised to be one of the party. Some unknown men, were presented to me as inspectors as they were called, and we journeyed together to the castle, we have just left. Here our fine expedition shewed itself. In the cellar and subterraneous windings of the castle, a mint was raised, and we coined away to our hearts' delight.

Ferrandino. Then you were false coiners?

Nero. At least our coins were not so good as they should be, although it was very difficult to discover that they were false.—We have worked away at it diligently, and the whole country must swarm with base Venetian zechins and dollars with Roman zechins, Turkish coins of all sorts, and with curious gold pieces which bear republican arms, and are not worth a doit.—This fabric they have at length detected and have sent soldiers to destroy the coining nest—We have sent away fine fat gold barrels! Toroners, the steward of the castle, generally received them quarterly and sent them further.

Ferrandino. Aha! now I can interpret, what that was the steward loaded in wagons at night, and carried away.

Nero. Yes, a transport was despatched to-night. Probably he was the convoy has fallen into the hands of the Venetian soldiers, and it may then chance to go a little hard with their throats.

Ferrandino. And where is the money carried to?

Nero. Where else, but to the Prince Nickanor?

Ferrandino. Damnation !

Nero. Who knows if they have not already whispered something in his ear. Had you been in the castle, when it was possessed by the soldiers, you too would not have run much more—Your curiosity, your intrepidity, which would have brought another in trouble, has saved you.

Ferrandino. You have delivered me from the greatest danger, and I hope a time will come, when I can testify, my gratitude.

Nero. Do not speak of it ! I have already been so long in your debt that I am very happy it was in my power to repay you something.—All we must now think of is where we shall turn ourselves and what we shall do ?

It was midnight, when Rodosla came crawling back between the bushes. He was loaded and cried out to them.

"Is it not true, you are hungry ? I bring you something and—It is not a great deal but, yet it is something and therefore better than nothing. I could not get more in the hurry,"

"You are a fellow, like gold !"—cried Nero.

"Only not like any of ours"—said Rodosla, laughing.

Nero. Well ? how does it look ?

Rodsla. It looks badly. By as much as I have discovered, the soldiers have caught the steward and his transport, have surprised the castle, will probably search it, and find the precious machinery, and all of our good friends that fall into their hands will have but little occasion to care for a hempen chain of favor.

Nero. That we may suppose!

Rodosla. But that I may not forget one in the other!—When I was about to join you with my provision, I met a young fellow, who crept round about the castle like cats round hot milk.—I examined him and soon found that he was strange here. We entered into conversation, and he related to me what he knew of the expediton of the soldiers to the castle. In doing this he bewailed his master, who, as he said was in the castle and was perfectly innocent of all. I asked him to describe him, and by his description I should suppose this gentleman is the Signor Ferrandino as he called him.

Ferrandino. I am—Where is the fellow.

Rodosla. I shewed him a hole, where he will await my return, because I told him, I should most likely be able to bring him tidings of his master.

Ferrandino. Bring him to me, noble Rodosla! it must be Ludovico.

Nero. Ludovico?

Ferrandino. I expected his arrival.

Rodosla. He shall be here immediately! He crawled off and soon returned followed by Ludovico.

He gave a loud shout when he saw his captain and his old comrade Nero.

What questions were then asked, now a recital, now answer, and they for a moment forgot their unfavorable situation.

But when these moments were passed, they began to deliberate on it, and there was then much thought and spoken.

" Now let me speak too!" said Rodosla who till then had sat there very quiet.—" I do not at all know, who this gentleman really is, but as he appears to be an old acquaintance of my comrade Nero, the proposition which I will make to him and you, cannot injure him. I propose that you should go with me to my brothers the Haiducks. The inhabitants of this country chiefly Venetians, have brought my countrymen down so low that they are obliged to dwell in uninhabited regions. We live like wolves in dens, we roam about betwen hanging rocks and inaccessible precipices, scramble from rock to rock like

goats, and must hunt our subsistence.
Continual fear, mortifying suspicion and
dreadful cares surround us and expose us to
the inclemency of every season. Often deprived of our requisite nourishment, we
must languish in gloomy caverns, or we
are reduced to hazard our life for our food.
Would it be a wonder if we were inhuman,
but we are not ; and always tormented by
the sensibility of our miserable condition,
spare the habitations of our enemies, who
are the authors of our misfortunes, rob only
in the greatest necessity, and to keep ourselves from starving. We kill only in our
defence, and do not burn down villages.
We sometimes take an ox from the pastur-
age of the villager, and drag it to our dens,
we cannot starve. Hunger is painful ! we
need the flesh for our food and the skins
for our shoes. These are one of the just
necessaries of our wretched existence,
since we are doomed to wander in the most
rugged regions, regions covered neither by
grass or earth, but every where sharp pointed rocks—our adversities endue us with
courage. But we treat him who is not
our enemy, humanely and with more gen-
erosity than we are treated by our perse-
cutors. Will you dwell among such people

Ferrandino, after a pause, said—

'Lead me to your unfortunate brethren—
I follow you."

Before Rodosla cou'd reply, Ferrandino
continued brisk and lively.

"At spirit which from me, at this moment returns. My determination is fixed.
Perhaps I shall be to you and your brethren
what you little dream of. Are they brave,
they shall find in me a leader, who is firmly
resolved to reinstate them in those rights,
of which they have been so unjustly robbed."

"Will you do that?"—said Rodosla,
and fixed his eyes on him.

"Should I fall,"—continued Ferrandino
in full animation,—" I will fall for you and
my death will be honorable. I have risked
my life for inferior, more trifling, and often
not very honorable things, I will now venture it to redress the unfortunate, who, by
unjust persecutions are banished in soli-
tudes, in the dens of grief and wretchedness. I will assemble your brethren round
about me, will animate their courage, will
breathe bravery and perseverance into their
souls, will stand at their head and ask their
pursuers : Will you be humane towards
human beings. Will you no longer expose
and abandon them to merciless hunger and
misery ? will you give them shelter among
you ?—And if they say no—

"See, Rodosla! that I will do this, that I will assert all this with you, I solemnly swear by the Almighty God above us. I give you my word; and Rinaldini is accustomed to keep his word."

'Rinaldini?"—said Rodosla, surprised and confounded.

"He stands before you,"—said Ferrandino.

"At last, captain!"—said Ludovico,—" we shall yet once more through your resolution, return to our suitable places.— Wandering about in the world of women and of mystery is not for such men as we are. Women heat the head, and mysteries cool the heart. At most they inspire you with but love, thereby we gain nothing. We must stand open, man against man, eye to eye, and must either fall with noise, or remain standing."

As the evening was approaching, they removed themselves further up to a cave, of which they took possession. Rodosla took it upon himself to procure provision, crept down the valley and returned well laden. He had been so careful as to purchase a mantle from a Morlack for Ferrandino, whom this attention so well pleased, that he repayed him threefold for it

At night they encamped in the cave and

Ludovico was so joyed to return to his former way of living, that he was concerned about nothing but how to bring every thing to its former condition.

Ferrandino gave himself up to meditation, recalled to his memory his past life, and mustered up the most possible incidents of futurity

BOOK VI

At day-break Ferrandino's three com
panions went out to reconnoitre, At noon
they would return with provisions, for Ferrandino resolved not to leave the cave till
he had received certain intelligence of the
soldiers' departure from the castle.

His companions were gone and lay mu-
sing in the cave, when he heard a noise at
a little distance, that was approaching
nearer and nearer. He drew himself back
to the darkness of the cave and listened.
At length he saw something wave by the
entrance—He advanced, went out of the
cave and perceived sideways between
thorns and briars a human figure who, appeared to be seeking stones or herbs or
at least to be buised with something on the
ground. When he raised himself Ferrandino saw that it was a tall, strong figure

clothed in skins, with pale countenance and long beard. He went forward and cried out : who's there ?—quickly flew the savage, like a roused deer, over rocks and clifts, and was soon hid from his sight by hills and bushes.

" Undoubtedly an unfortunate or a criminal driven by despair or guilt among these dens and precipices—" sighed Ferrandino and retreated into his cave.

Here he had lain, long pondering and meditating, when he heard the voice of men. He listened : the voices approached, he seized his arms. Nero and Ludovico entered the cave.

They were well laden with provision, amunition and arms, which they had purchased.—Towards noon Rodosla also appeared.

" I have" said he, " learnt, as certain, that sixteen soldiers are yet in the castle but who will also withdraw to-morrow. They have exercised speedy and rigid justice, for I saw four men cut down from the trees before the castle. A proof that it has gone a little severe."

" I am particularly interested,"—said Ferrandino—" by the fate of only a single person in the castle."

" And this is ?"—said Rodosla.

" A girl—"

" Aha !"—said Ludovico—" I could have guessed as much."

" Margalisa, the sister of the steward, who was the companion of my solitude in the castle, and whose unhappiness, if any misfortune should befall her, I should hartily lament. She is innocent and knew nothing of the subterraneous secrets of the castle."

Rodosla now made the proposition he would go to some of his brothers in the mountans, would speak to them, and agree upon the place which they would first make themselves masters of.

This proposal was approved of, and Rodosla immediately set out upon the way You will now—said Ludovico—soon again be captain, and we shall again be feared. Hitherto we crept precariously through the world, but now the old jovial life will return.

Ferrandino. I expect it.

Ludovico. And I swear it

Ferrandino. O ! That a man—

Ludovico. Is a man. Does he not forget this, nothing but what is human can happen to him. And then the worst of it is, if it is bad, death.

Ludovico. Oh ! death stares one in the face every where ; It is the prospect on

the stage of human life, which, is repre-
sented to us in every decoration. A cur-
tain, which, in the ancient Grecian style,
falls down, never rises   For all what death
seizes, he crushes down.

Ludovico. But he sometimes too ele-
vates.

Nero. That he does only to people of
our stamp, and then it is done *cum privile-
gio.*

Ludovico. We leave it to him.

Nero. Must we not ?

Ferrandino. What must a man not suffer ?. O fate ! fate ! how inflexibly do you
govern us ! and nevertheless I will not
give up my game for lost

Ludovico: Which?

A gun was just then discharged near the
cave in which they were holding their conversation. A roe, directly after, swiftly
bounded by, and a tall wild fellow followed.
Before the cave he stood still and mutter-
ed.

"But how could I miss !"

Nero softly approached him, took the
gun out of his hand backwards, and said :

"Comrade what do you want here ?"

The man amazed staggered a few paces
back, and said ;

"Who are you ?"

" That question to you—said Nero,"

"Return me my arms"—continued he
" I am a poor devil and this gun is all my
wealth, it must support me, my wife and
my children."

Ferrandino.   Fear not! your gun shall
be returned to you, if you are upright.

" What is your name ?"

Asan.   " My name is Nesta Asan."

Ferrandino.   Are you an Haiduk ?

Asan.   I am alas !

Nero.   Alas ?

Asan.   We are unfortunate men. Want
and misery sing to us the night-song, the
nuptial-song and the death-song.   Even
nature herself seems to be in compact with
mankind, to make us unhappy.   Behold
these regions in which we must live, do
they not appear to be more designed for
wild beasts than human beings? we live
among beasts, they clothe and nourish us,
while men treat us like brutes.

Ferrandino.   You have a wife ?

Asan.   A wife and dear little children,
who must fast to-day, since I have missed
the roe.

Ferrandino.   That they shall not.—There
take !—and here is money.

Asan.   What would you receive from
me for this money ? for one man will scarcely give any thing to another for nothing.

Ferrandino. What you receive from me is given disinterestedly. But if you will learn to know men, if you will live in their society, you may return to us.

Asan. How do you mean?

Ferrandino. We are gathering together your brethren, the oppressed Haiduks, to open battle against their enemies.

Asan. Will you do that?—Here is my hand. I will return and be one of you, I shall also bring brothers with me.

Ferrandino, They shall be welcome among us.

Asan. But may I ask, how it comes that you interes yourself in the cause of my brethren?

Ferrandino. It is the cause of humanity, which in me has given you an avenger.

Asan. And you are the avenger.

Ferrandino. I am.

Asan. Your name?

Ferrandino. Names do not make bad causes better nor good ones worse, but you shall know it. Perhaps you already know my name rather than myself, I am Rinaldini.

Asan. Rinaldini? and yet living?

Ferrandino. As you see.

Asan. You have a long time been reported dead.

Ferrandino. And I am not.

Asan. You will command us?

Ferrandino. Against your oppressors.

Asan. To-morrow you shall see me again, and as before said, I will not come singly.

Nero. Here is your gun. I have loaded it for you.

Ludovico. But when we stand in rank and file you will aim better

Asan. Never fear? I aim sure but to-day I missed, and lost my game to find you. The roe may run. What I have found here, is dearer to me—Adieu; renowned captain. He kissed Ferrandino's hand and skipped away.

The following day Rodosla seemed very pleased and exultingly cried out : "I have got quarters! we need only go." You will be received with joy.

He had scarcely spoke, when Asan appeared, followed by three armed men.

" Renowned captain!—said he,—I keep my word ; I come as you see, do not come singly.

" I am answerable for these three comrades as for myself. They all burn with desire, to fight under your command, and will convince you that they are the men you look for."

Ferrandino welcomed them. They silently gave him their hands. Rodosla spoke to them. They listened to him attentively. At length Asan said, " We have sent our wives and children to the interior of the mountains, and are ready to go, where Rinaldini leads."

The march was immediately resolved and entered upon. Their way led accross the mountains whose valleys they reached towards evening. They passed the night in a cavern in the rocks and the following morning arrived in the woods, in which Rodosla's friend and acquaintances awaited the arrival of the knights, whom he had promised to conduct,

Cheerful was the group, that expected him. A joyful shout welcomed him. All pressed towards Ferrandino, to kiss his hand, and Nestracamo, the eldest of the corps, ceremoniously saluted him with the following address.

" Welcome brave captain ! One, whose fame is proclaimed through nations, and penetrates even our inhospitable woods and mountains like an unerring arrow. welcome among the unhappy Haiduks ! What they can give and wish for your happiness they will give and wish sincerely, and the name of their deliverer will be uttered with gratitude by their children and children's children. We have been driven from the fine fruitful plains which our enemies possess, and chased like wild beasts into forests and wilderness : lead us from hence and let us retake what they have taken from us ; you shall be our prince and leader.

After this harrangue the women and children formed a circle round Ferrandino and danced about him to the tune of drums, trumpets, and triangles.—When the dance was finished, Ferrandino said :

" I come, you oppressed! to burst with you your chains. I will be your captain and fight your cause, vanquish or fall.

They conducted him to a tent and here they were deliberating and drinking till the stars twinkled in the heavens.

The following day he mustered his troop and found it one hundred and forty strong. Recrurters were sent out and in the space of three days Ferrandino saw himself at the head of three hundred warlike men. These he divided into three detachments. Nero commanded one Ludovico another, and Nestracamo the third.—He himself was commander-in-chief.

To secure a place of defence they resolved to possess themselves of the castle Ostosine That was done very easily, they attacked the castle, and made six Venetian soldiers, who lay in it, prisoners. Ferrandino immediately had the dungeon opened and released Margalisa, who that same day was to have been carried away to Trau, where the steward and his wife had already been taken. The good girl threw herself weeping into the arms of her knight, and sobbed:

'It is not a dream? I am free in your arms?''

"Aha!" said Ludovico, "the captain has already got something loving in his arms. He does nothing else!"

Margalisa was lost in a sort of joyful stuperfaction, which admits of so few reflections, that one scarcely enjoys half the present time, and in which it did not at all come into the castle? Enough, he was there and had loosened her chains. These thoughts filled her with gratitude, and she repeatedly called out, "I am thine! I am thine for ever"

By degrees he explained to her how and why he was come, and communicated to her his plan. She thought it excellent; and how could she otherwise? A little vanity too was mixed with her affection.—Ferrandino was about to make himself formidable and she was the beloved of this formidable man.

Feranaino took up his quarters in the castle, and as well as was possible in the hurry, fortified it, planted it with cannon, and sent forth detachments to scour the country.

At first they met with but little resistance. They possessed themselves of some places of defence, and collected money and provision together. They also increased in number and soon became five hundred strong.

But when the news of this sudden revolt of the Haiducks reached Trau, when it was known at Zara what was going forward; the governor immediately despatched an express to Venice, meanwhile he collected together his own forces, and consigned the command of it to a skilful general, who at the head of two thousand men advanced against the revolters.

Ferrandino soon received intelligence thereof. He occupied the castle, committed the garrison to the command of Nero, and advanced at the head of his men against the Venetians. He encamped in a narrow pass between the mountains of Lazara and awaited the enemy, who soon appeared.

"What moves you," said the general, "to a revolt against your superiors?"

"The Haiduks," replied Ferrandino,

"are urged to this by the cruelty of their oppressors. They drive them from house and home, from fields and meadows, which belong to their forefathers, and chase them among wild beasts in wildernesses. They persecute them even there? in those regions of wretchedness and hunger, daily and hourly do not suffer them to live at rest among brutes, laugh at their misery, and endeavour wholly to extripate them. That is the reason of this created insurrection—give them back what you have robbed them of, and they will lay down their arms."

"The Haiduks," returned the general, "are robbers. They plunder the caravans of the Turks and, christians with equal pleasure, and cannot live among good men If they do not immediately lay down their arms, they shall all be cut to pieces without mercy!"

To this he received no answer.—He once more repeated, "lay down your arms."

Ferrandino answered him briefly,

"Fetch them."

At that the colonel asked him:

"Who is he, that speaks so boldly to me?"

The answer was:

"It is Rinaldini that speaks to you."

With this he gave the signal of attack and fighting drove the Venetians down the coast to Slafileo, where the remainder threw themselves into the castle.

The ensuing day, the Venetians having received reinforcements, resumed the attack, and the Haiduks oppressed oy superior numbers fled in all directions.

Ferrandino. I reckoned too much on the known courage of the Haiduks. Are they not the same, of whom only three or four often attack whole caravans, who would encounter sixteen, or twenty Turks, and put them to flight?

Ludovico. They fought like lions and the Venetians have left more than four hundred men laying in the field, but they wanted a leader. They fought in small detachments and in the whole it came to nothing.—But had you been among us it would have gone quite different.

Ferrandino. I still intend to return to you to-day, and you return to me defeated.

Ludovico. A cursed piece of business! I do not expect succour and here they will starve us out.—We ought now to think on nothing else than our retreat.

Ferrandino. That will always be left to us.

Meanwhile Rodosla returned from his

mission, and comforted them with the expectation of succour through the means of Nectracamo—Ferandino sent out some courageous men from his garrison towards him and on the third day the Haiduks appeared in the field. The Venetians went out against them and a bloody battle ensued.—Ferrandino made use of this moment and at the head of forty men sallied from the castle on the encampment of the Venetians. But he found the enemy stronger than he expected, and saw himself with his company quickly surrounded—Here nothing but flight could save him. Fighting he cut a passage to the castle. Ludovico and Nero fell by his side ; of the forty but five returned to the castle.

"Now am I lost!"—said he to himself, "I feel it.—Ludovico and Nero my brave comrades fell by my side. My supporters are sunk and I shall sink after them."

Without delay he provided himself with jewels and arms, desired Margalisa to clothe herself in male-attire, and accompained by her, hurried through the cellars and bye-way out of the castle.

Through the whole of a moonlight night they scrambled about between rocks and cliffs and with day break reached the former city of Salona.—From here they easily

reached Spalatra, where they found a corn-
bark, but which was only bound for Curzola. With this they embarked.

The arrived at the Island, and Ferrandino alighted at the house of the captain's
brother, who rented a farm two hours distant from the city of Curzola, and carried
on a considerable coal-trade. This man
informed Ferrandino, that he was a Milan-
ese and designed to visit the islands of the
Adriatic and Mediterranean seas, as he
had already wandered through all Italy and
could gain but little account of them.

"Yes," continued the coal-merchant,
"that is certain! he who once begins to
travel can never leave off. I have already
made this remark on many travellers. Our
clergyman compares travelling to a forbid-
den fruit; the further it hangs from us the
more we long for it."

Ferrandino did not dispute it. For a
few days he lived quietly in his house, and
then visited the most remarkable places of
the island, and with the first opportunity
embarked for Meleda.

On their passage the captain informed
him that a Turkish or Grecian Prince having got into some difficulty at Ragusa, had
been conducted hither where he must remain till the verdict of the Senate decided

his fate, under whose acknowledged protection Ragusa principally stands, and whose decision he has called upon him.

- Ferrandino was more interested in this relation than the captain believed. This prince he thought could be no other than Nikanor, the wise old man of Fronteia With uncommon expectations he entered the harbour, alighted and hastened to the residence of the prince.

It lay in a lonely valley between mountains, was not splendid, but yet cheerful and pleasant. He approached with panting heart, and found every thing around, still and lonely, he perceived Fabio at the gate, who had scarcely discovered him, when he clasped his hands in amazement and hurried into the house. Ferrandino followed him on foot, crossed a small hall, opened a chamber and beheld the old man before him. Joyfully he flew to meet him and in a tone of friendship said :

" Welcome Ferrandino !"

Ferrandino. Here ? here do I find you ?

Nikanor. Here do I see you ?

Ferrandino. You have left Ragusa ?

Nikanor. As you see.

Ferrandino. I cannot guess—

Nikanor. Why I have done so ?

Ferrandino. Just so.

Nikanor. You shall soon know all.—
I rejoice to see you safe. I already believe
you to be in the hands of the Venetians.
As it is, it is better for us both, and I thank
Heaven for your deliverance!—How did
you escape out of Ostrosine?

Ferrandino related what befell him and
what we have already been made acquainted with. The old man shook his head,
and said :

Singular man ! To Corsica you would
not go, and at that time threw us all into
confusion, yet at the head of the impotent
Haiduks you voluntarily exposed yourself,
and hazarded your life for vagabonds !

Ferrandino. Their condition is to be
pitied.

Nikanor. So is that of the Corsicans.—
Rather say, your own embarrassment led
you to them, and, into fresh embarrassments.

Ferrandino. Where was there ever a
place in the world, on which I stood without embarrassment ?—My whole life has
been only a chain of difficulties, and still is
even at the moment I stand before you.

Nikanor. I guess what you would say—
you reckon your embarrassments to mine.
Is it not so ?

Ferrandino. That you may suppose.

Nickanor. But I am not embarrassed.

Ferrandino. Not?

Nikanor. No.

Ferrandino. And yet—

Nikanor. Believe me, I am not embarrassed.

Ferrandino. But you have left Ragusa?

Nikanor. Because they would offend me there. E.t : will he shown, .hat——Enough ! you shall know all The sun though obsc.red by clouds is nevertheless the sun.——But at present salute your friend !

As he said this, he opened a side-aoor, and Ferrandino entered the chamber, in which he found Olympia.

She hurried towards him, imprinted kisses of welcome on his brow, and rejoiced to see him again. He seized. her hand, fixed his eyes upon her, and significantly asked :

"You have left Ragusa ?"

Olympia. As one leaves a faithless lover.

Ferrandino With vexation and disgust.

Olympia. And with contempt.

Ferrandino. With contempt ?—You?—

Olympia. We—The prince has been injured and expects the satisfaction that the high court of justice will give him.

Ferrandino. Will they ?

Olympia. They must and will.—A company of false coiners have been discovered in castle Ostrosine, belonging to the Countess Vendramino, and they have arrested the countess.—

Ferrandino. Did she know that they harboured in the castle?

Olympia. I do not know.—Prince Nikanor is an acquaintance of the Countess's, and they think so ignobly of him as to believe he too is not without a knowledge of the imposture. His rank and condition protect him from public insult; but they have also arrested his friend the senator Protega.

Ferrandino. The senator too?

Olympia. The prince sends his retinue to Cyprus, writes to the high court, and accompanied by only me, Fabio, and a few domestics, journeys hither. Here we daily expect a courier from the grand Sultan.

Ferrandino. From himself?

Olympia. From himself.

Ferrandino. Tell me also, who is the prince?

Olympia. That he will tell you himself. The mask must now fall, and you will learn secrets that will fill you with astonishment.

Fabio now entered the chamber, and requested them, in the name of Nikanor, to come to dinner quested them, in the name of Nikanor, to come to dinner.

At table the old man discoursed very composedly on various subjects, but not a word of himself. He also requested Ferrandino to relate his adventures at castle Ostrosine and with the Haiduks; and when he had finished, laughingly asked,

"And what became of your Margalisa?"

Ferrandino. She has followed me.

Olympia. Followed you?

Nikanor. And is here with you?

Ferrandino. In male attire she has followed me to this place.

The old man rang the bell and when the servant entered, desired :

"That his guest's page should be well entertained."

When the servant had received his orders and left the room, he continued :

"Serena and Serafina, are gone together to Cyprus."

Ferrandino. And Nikanor——?

Nikanor. Asks you if you will stop with him and share his fate, or if you will go further.

Ferrandino. I will remain with you.

Nikanor. 'Tis well! But if——. Yet of that we can speak another time. But I read in your looks a certain curiosity, regarding me and my *being*. Is it not so?"

Ferrandino. Then you will at length tell me————

Nikanor. What you wish to know. Though not at this moment, but sooner than you will expect it. I await despatches from Constantinople. Before I open them you shall know who I am.

Olympia. We are in hourly expectation of their arrival.

Nikanor. Meanwhile Ferrandino with us will wait with patience.

After the repast Ferrandino was shown to a chamber, and Margalisa came to him.

"It appears," said she, "that we shall remain here?"

Ferrandino. For the present.—Yes.

Margalisa. You may go where you will I follow you. I have no longer a paternal roof, I have no asylum. Your residence must be mine for the future. Or would you be so cruel as to abandon me ? could you do that ?

Ferrandino. No, Margalisa ? you shall remain with me. But you will never see your Morlacks again.

Margalisa. If I but see you I shall always see what I love to see most. You are more to me than all the Morlacks in the whole world !

You are my Probatino and I am your Posestrema for ever.

In the evening Ferrandino supped alone with Margalisa. The old man sent him some books and Olympia a guitar. To this she wrote : " A girl you have with you and I send you a guitar, I know that you cannot be happy without them."

The morn of the following day was too enchanting to be left unenjoyed by him. Ferrrandino left Margalisa sleeping and hastened out. Ferrandino mounted a hill and surveyed the country. The mist lay yet in the valley. It slowly ascended whirling by the mountains like columns of water. The sun rose above the ocean in dazzling splendor. The exulting tones of the feathered songsters was heard from a thousand different throats. It ascended above the tops of the mountains, and stood in its utmost splendor in the serene blue heavens.

In how many different situations hast thou. O King of Heaven! already beheld me. Thy beneficent rays descend on me in cheerful regions, as in deserts, and always hast thou found me like a fugitive, wandering from place to place. Ah! when will you present your cheering looks to me where I can enjoy them : Here I, celebrate your arrival in undisturbed tranquillity!

As he said this he threw himself under a towering cypress, and lost himself in deep contemplation. From the foot of the hill resounded the shrill cry of a shepherdess. He looked down into the valley, and was witness of a lovely morning-scene.

A nimble-footed country lass laden with a basket, approached the shepherd and brought him his breakfast. They joked and toyed with one another, and smiled at a young man who was coming towards them with a lute under his arm.

"Where are you rambling to again?" said the girl.

"I have brought my Dorilis some morning music," said the lute-player, and sat himself by them.

He immediately played a prelude to a duetto, and the girl and her shepherd did not require much pressing to sing.

Ferrandino was just about to express his approbation openly to the songsters, when he perceived Margalisa. So attentively had he listened, that she was quite near him.

"The old gentleman," said she, "is looking for you every where. Has sent all his people out after you. Some strange Turkish men are arrived."

On hearing this Ferrandino forgot the tribute which he intended to have made to the singers, and hastened with Margalisa to the dwelling of the old man Nikanor.

He received him cordially in his chamber. Olympia only was with him.

" The despatches are arrived from Constantinople,"—said he. " They are as yet unopened. I am ignorant of their contents. I remember my promise and the time is come when I shall fulfill it—Seat yourself!"

Ferrandino seated himself on a sofa, and the old man began.

" The Prince Anselmo Gonzago urged his courage, contrary to his fathers will and wish, in the war. He served, without making himself known, as a nobleman, and took the field as a volunteer in a campaign against the Turks. In a hot engagement he was wounded and taken prisoner.—By chance the Serasqueer saw him. His mien pleased him; he interested himself in his fate, had him cured, and sent him to the grand Vizier.—He found as much pleasure in his prisoner as the Serasqueer; often entertained himself with him, wondered at his knowledge, his understanding, and was charmed with his open countenance.

" The Sultan at that time visiting the army was presented by the Vizier with his prisoner. He was also received into grace with the sovereign, who took him, at his return from the army, with him to Constantinople.

"I will avoid all prolixity; for these despatches wait to be broke open.—To be brief, therefore Anselmo became the favorite and confidante of the Sultan.

"In Adrianople he found means to get more closer acquainted with the sister of the Sultan than he should have been. The effects of this forbiden intercourse soon became visible, and Fardinia and Anselmo ventured to throw themselves at the feet of the Sultan, and to make him privy to their happiness and misfortune. The Sultan was at first hurrid away by a torrent of anger, and had already drawn his sabre to plunge them into eternity, when Fardina called out to him from the Koran :" God is merciful and man is his image—" The Sultan restrained himself, sheathed his sword, and pronounced to them their condemnation.

"Anselmo, who discovered his condition, was delivered to a Venetian galley and went to Malta where he took the cross. Fardina was banished to Syria. At Damascus she was delivered of a son whom the Bassa committed to a priest, who had him educated, and when he was eight years old sent him to Greece. Here he was entrusted to a learned man, in whom was concentrated the wisdom of the ancients and moderns and who found his pupil as eager for instruction as he could wish.

"At the age of seventeen he went on a journey with his teacher. They traversed all Greece, went to Egypt, ranged the sandy deserts, admired the grandeur of the pyramids, and visited even the Temple of Ammon."

"What?" exclaimed Ferrandino, eagerly.

"You would say interrupted the old man "What? are you then this travelling youth who saw the Temple of Ammon?—I answer you: I am. I am Nikanor, the son of the Sultaness Fardina."

After a short pause he continued his naration :—

"I was in my twentieth year when my teacher delivered me to the Bassa of Damascus. He unfolded to me the secret of my birth and brought me to my mother. A short time after, she died in these arms and left me her possessions."

Here he covered his face, and when he uncovered it again tears glistened in his eyes. Ferrandino afflicted cast his eyes on the ground.—The old man collected himself and proceeded :—

"I left Syria, traveled through India, Persia, and at last went to Europe. In my six and twentieth year I became acquainted with my father at Malta. He provided me with recommendations and I went to Rome : alas ! the news of his death followed me there.

"In Rome, in one of the first houses, I became acquainted with a lady whom her parents designed for the convent. We saw and loved each other. The vigilance of her parents was baffled, and we were happy to be unhappy. Her brothers took upon themselves, as they said, the honour of their house, and I was so unfortunate as to kill one in a duel, after having severely wounded the other. I fled to Venice to elude the pursuits of the enraged family, who threatened the most dreadful vengeance. I went to France, traversed Spain and Portugal and six years after returned to Italy. In Venice I learned that my Laura had become the mother of a son, he was, as was said, sent into the country, and the mother was placed in a convent. For twelve years I sought wife and child in vain. At length fortune permitted me to speak to Laura, but my son had disappeared. With fatherly affection I sought him every where, and at length was so fortunate as to find him.—Yes! I found him. But where?—Alas I found him at the head of a Banditti of Robbers."

" Great God!" cried Ferrandino.

The old man composedly proceeded :

" You—you, yourself are my son. Now explain to yourself all what I did and what I could not do for you. The confession which I made in writing saved your life the last time at Ragusa."

Ferrandino fell on his neck with emotion. Tears intermingled with tears, and a solemn pause interrupted their loud discourse.

The old man recovered his composure the first, squeezed his hand and said:—

" You were, and still are my son.—Never shall you leave me again,—we will receive our sentence together. The Ragusians demand my life ; yours is in danger, and should we fall, father and son can die together "

He rose up, and desired that the Tartars who had brought him the despatches of the Sultan should enter. In their presence he touched his forehead with the packet, bowed profoundly, and broke the seal.

He unfolded the letter of the Vizier, read

the writings of the Sultan, and said,—

"I am appointed Bashaw of Cyprus."

He held the unfolded letter opposite the Tartars. They fell down, kissed the garment of the old man, and said:

"We accompany the Bashaw of the most high and splendid Porte, to Cyprus."

The old man turned himself with inquiring looks to his son. He fell into his arms and Olympia said,—

Now you will indeed be happy and at rest.

The following day they embarked for Cyprus.

THE END

Lightning Source UK Ltd.
Milton Keynes UK
UKHW030607200519
342983UK00007B/873/P